The Lada
International
Speedway
Book

The Lada International Speedway Book

Edited by Richard Bott

Stanley Paul / London Melbourne Sydney
Auckland Johannesburg

Contents

ACKNOWLEDGEMENTS
The editor would like to thank *Speedway Star* photographers Mike Patrick and Trevor Meeks for providing the majority of the excellent photographs used in the *Lada International Speedway Book*. Other contributors include Wright Wood and *Speedway Mail* photographer Alf Weedon. He is indebted, particularly, to *Speedway Star* editor Philip Rising, Ken Robinson and Frank Auffret who promoted the first British Supporters Speedway Convention, in Blackpool last November, and for allowing him to use material from that convention. Thanks are due also to Lada Cars for their considerable support, particularly Advertising and Promotions Executive David Usher.

Stanley Paul & Co. Ltd

An imprint of the Hutchinson Publishing Group

17–21 Conway Street, London W1P 6JD

Hutchinson Group (Australia) Pty Ltd
30–32 Cremorne Street, Richmond South, Victoria 3121
PO Box 151, Broadway, New South Wales 2007

Hutchinson Group (NZ) Ltd
32–34 View Road, PO Box 40–086, Glenfield, Auckland 10

Hutchinson Group (SA) (Pty) Ltd
PO Box 337, Bergvlei 2012, South Africa

First published 1982
©Richard Bott 1982

ISBN 0 09 149581 4

Right **Sweden's Jan Andersson receives the 'King of the Concrete' Match Race trophy from Mrs David Hunt at Wembley Arena**
Below **England had another triumph under Len Silver. They beat Denmark in a short series. Erik Gundersen and Dave Jessup duel for the lead at Hackney**

RICHARD BOTT

Chief northern sports writer of the *Sunday Express*. Edited the *Champions Book of Speedway* series and the *Peter Collins Speedway Book* series for Stanley Paul. Also co-authored the controversial *Speedway Grand Slam*. Chairman of the Speedway Writers and Photographers' Association. Former business manager of ex-world champion Peter Collins. Covers speedway for the *Daily Express*, under the pen-name 'Dick Julian', and for the *Sunday Express*, though his main duties are as a football correspondent.

Bruce Penhall . . . the young American who thrilled a 92,000 World final crowd at Wembley last September

Introduction
by Richard Bott

My favourite sport breaks new ground in 1982 with the staging of the World Individual Championship final in Los Angeles. Twelve years ago, when Stanley Paul published my first *Champions Book of Speedway*, the odds against a world final in America were phenomenal.

The last few years may have seen the recession bring a few dark clouds into focus but the silver lining has been the re-emergence of so many ambitious and talented young riders from the other side of the 'pond'.

Suddenly, we have an American world champion again . . . a young, handsome thrill-maker called Bruce Penhall. His triumph at Wembley Stadium last September, in front of 92,000 ecstatic fans, may have been disappointing for England as host nation but Penhall's riding was so spectacular that no one could deny him his moment of glory.

Speedway has always been an international sport and America had a lot to say in its pioneering days back in the twenties and thirties. Jack and Cordy Milne, Wilbur Lamoreaux and 'Sprouts' Elder are legendary names in Speedway's 'Hall of Fame'. But the World Championship, won by Jack Milne in 1937 at Wembley, has never been staged in the USA . . . until now.

And providing a golden link with a glorious heritage is the fact that Jack Milne is to help promote the 1982 world final at the Los Angeles Memorial Coliseum.

Another world final, the pairs championship, will be raced in Australia in December, a further link with the past. It was in Australia, in 1923, that speedway laid down its roots and ever since then young men from the land of the kangaroo have come to Britain to race in the finest speedway league in the world.

So speedway is stretching out in 1982, spreading its wings, taking two of its major finals beyond the frontiers of Europe for the first time.

And as the sport becomes more ambitious and expansive it is thanks largely to a company which reflects these same progressive qualities, **LADA CARS**, that I have been able to compile a new speedway book and Stanley Paul has been able to publish it. Lada involved themselves in speedway only a few years ago and, like all potential sponsors, they were looking for a suitable platform to advertise their wares.

Their bold, progressive outlook has been aptly rewarded. They took a considerable gamble in providing financial backing for the first indoor speedway meeting at Wembley Arena in 1979. That event has now become a firm fixture in the speedway calendar.

Now they are backing the first *Lada International Speedway Book* and the accent is

7

Penhall in action – and out in front! The American star leads Sweden's Richard Hellsen, England's Chris Morton and Denmark's Erik Gundersen during the World Team Cup round at King's Lynn

on the word 'international'. My guest contributors are **Bruce Penhall** (USA), **Kenny Carter** (England), **Hans Nielsen** (Denmark), **Ivan Mauger** (New Zealand) and **Jan Andersson** (Sweden).

My last book, *Speedway Grand Slam*, has been called 'the most controversial speedway book ever written'. In some quarters it was not well received because controversy usually involves criticism and people are sensitive to such views. But without controversy and criticism, without straight talking and harsh facts, complacency takes root.

Some of the items in the *Lada International Speedway Book* are controversial, critical, aggressive, outspoken. They are not necessarily my views but they are about speedway issues that concern all of us.

England's disappointing year, following their unprecedented feats in 1980, was knee-deep in controversy. Michael Lee was never out of the headlines – but was he as 'black' as he was painted? Len Silver, who

took over as England's team manager, was pilloried for our defeat in the World Cup. Was it fair that he should be made the scapegoat?

After the incredible scenes at Vojens, where rain held up the Inter-continental final for 95 minutes, and the riders were overruled when they asked for a postponement, the question has to be asked: do referees gamble with riders' lives?

Is British speedway heading for possible bankruptcy as Ivan Mauger suggests? If it is, has he the right to criticize when he has earned more money than anyone from the British promoters?

Is the 50-points rule, introduced into the National League regulations in 1982, going to be as farcical as management committee member Ian Thomas suggests?

Controversy? Yes. And plenty of it. But I hope I have managed to maintain a healthy balance in the arguments; and that the first *Lada International Speedway Book* will entertain and inform you.

Lada's stake in Speedway
by David Usher

Advertising and Promotions
Manager, Lada Cars GB Ltd

Hull Vikings . . . Newcastle Diamonds . . . Ivan Mauger . . . the Lada Indoor International at Wembley Arena . . . yes, we've had quite a stake in speedway in the last four years – and we would like a bigger one!

We have had super exposure out of speedway and that's the name of the game when you are a sponsor.

Our involvement began in 1976, with the last Russian tour of British League tracks, when we were asked to sponsor the Soviet team.

We went around the tour venues – Wolverhampton, Reading, Belle Vue, Sheffield, Swindon and Exeter – and liked what we saw . . . an exciting sport with loads of appeal and, potentially, an excellent vehicle for marketing our name and product.

Ten years ago nobody had heard of Lada Cars in Britain, and it has been a slow process creating an awareness of the name LADA. But speedway has helped considerably.

After that Russian tour we had talks with Ian Thomas and Brian Larner, the promoters at Hull. We import our cars through Hull Docks to our British base at Bridlington. So it was logical, if we were going to get involved with a British track, to pick the local one. Hull became the LADA VIKINGS in 1979, the first fully commercially-sponsored team in the British League.

The highlight of that first season came in September when two of the Hull riders rode in the World Championship final in Poland, Ivan Mauger taking his sixth world title and the eighteen-year-old American, Kelly Moran, finishing a very creditable fourth.

The big disappointment was the Lada Vikings missing out on the British League championship in the very last match of the season. And they were also pipped for the *Speedway Star* Knock-out Cup in a two-legged final against Cradley Heath.

But, generally, Hull had an exciting year. Lada Cars were delighted to be part of it.

Our involvement in speedway increased in the winter of 1979 when we sponsored the first-ever indoor meeting in Britain . . . the Lada Indoor International at Wembley Arena. After three years this event has now become part of the speedway calendar.

Again, it was Ian and Brian who offered it to us. We went along to Wembley to have a look and liked the idea. It was new, different. We felt it would catch on.

Above **Lada Cars sponsored two British teams in 1981. Here is the Newcastle Lada Diamonds line-up. Back row** (*left to right*)**: Robbie Blackadder, Alan Emerson, Dave Younghusband (team manager), Rod Hunter, Kym Mauger. Front: David Bargh, Derek Richardson and Keith Bloxsome**

The first meeting was, well, 'joke' isn't quite the word. But it was a good laugh, the accent being on fun rather than serious speedway. Since then the racing has improved considerably and the riders do take it seriously. So, although we are not sure which direction the meeting should take from now on, the Lada Indoor International at Wembley is certainly here to stay – and we love being involved with it.

In 1980 we expanded our sponsorship by taking on Newcastle Diamonds in the National League. It was a natural progression. It gave us a team in each league and with Newcastle being Ian Thomas's other track and the geographical situation being suitable, we were quite prepared to give the Diamonds our support. Another important factor was that we had a good Lada dealer in the area.

I mentioned earlier that we have had good exposure from speedway. Sponsoring a team in each league has been very rewarding because the riders wear LADA race jackets wherever they race in team competition. That enables us to advertise our name all over the country.

In addition, our local dealers can promote themselves at their tracks and, in Hull and Newcastle, the riders have helped promote Lada Cars by making personal appearances.

It's very sad that Hull are not operating in the British League in 1982, as a result of their dispute with the Rugby League Football Club who are the landlords of the Boulevard Stadium.

But we have Newcastle and the Indoor International, we have our individual tie-up with Ivan Mauger, one of the greatest riders of all time, and we have the *Lada International Speedway Book*. In addition, we are involving ourselves in the 1982 World championship.

There can be no question that, through our sporting involvement, we have established the name LADA in Great Britain. We have sponsored golf, basketball, horse racing, rally driving and snooker.

Some people do abuse a sponsorship. They tend to take the money and run. But we have very few complaints about speedway.

Mind you, there was one rider who abused his Lada car to the extent that, when the number plate fell off, he took a hammer and two six-inch nails to replace it. He managed to break the steering wheel off on one occasion and on another there was more oil in the boot than the engine!

Also, we were not happy about certain newspaper reports when two Hull riders broke down en route to a crucial meeting during the 1979 season. The reports implied that the riders in question had been driving Lada cars and that the breakdowns

Left **The Lada Indoor International at Wembley Arena has become an annual gala day for fans starved of speedway during the winter months. This picture from the 1981 meeting shows England's Chris Morton fighting to hold off three other international stars, Erik Gundersen, Jim McMillan and Hans Nielsen**

Lada Cars promotions executive David Usher is interviewed by Richard Bott at the *Speedway Star*
speak-in at Blackpool

had cost Hull the British League championship. The riders were not driving Lada cars because very few members of the Hull team were provided with one.

Generally, we feel that speedway riders, promoters and supporters are a super bunch and we would like to take this opportunity to thank, in particular, the supporters' clubs at Hull and Newcastle.

If we have a criticism of speedway it is that the commercial promotion of the sport is not as good as it should be. Individually, the promoters and riders are great to deal with. It is when they all get together that the problems start. I believe there is a dire need for the BSPA to appoint a full-time promotions executive.

Some time ago, when the British League was 'up for grabs' when Gulf Oil ended their sponsorship, we were quite seriously interested in taking over and spent a good deal of time and effort talking to the BSPA's representative. We heard nothing more . . . which amazes us!

Speedway has done a lot for Lada cars. We like the sport and the people in it. And we are willing to talk to anybody who comes up with a sensible and serious proposition . . . because we would like to do more.

Wasn't Wembley wonderful?

Sunday Express *sports writer* **Richard Bott**, *who reported on his first World Championship in 1960, recalls one of speedway's greatest finals . . . Saturday 5 September 1981, the night an American bobby-dazzler won over a Wembley crowd with an electrifying display.*

Dave Jessup, Kenny Carter and Erik Gundersen will not agree with the title of this chapter and doubtless I could add the names of Michael Lee, Ole Olsen and a few more. But fate always makes somebody suffer before raising the hand of the victor.

And the most important feature of the 1981 World Championship was not that it produced a great champion but a great final, an occasion to lift the depression of a crisis-torn season, when almost every British track lost money; a memorable and marvellous advertisement for the sport.

The 92,000 of us lucky enough to be at Wembley, poured out of the old stadium burbling about the drama and daring, our heads spinning with excitement. And not long afterwards, millions more shared those same thrills on television.

I have lost count of the number of people who have come up to me since that Wembley night and said: 'I never rated speedway until I saw that world final on TV. Fabulous stuff. An American chap won it, didn't he?'

Yes. And that American chap was, of course, Bruce Lee Penhall. And considering he took the title from an English world champion and destroyed the hopes of three other home contenders, the reception he was given by the Wembley crowd was staggering.

Penhall's popularity has never been in doubt. Nor has his talent. He didn't start favourite for nothing. But it was the way he won that brought Wembley to its feet in a great stamping, shouting, trumpet-blowing celebration.

The golden-haired twenty-four-year-old Californian glamour boy – a journalistic cliché but it says it all! – produced two incredible neck-or-nothing photo-finishes to grab vital extra points from the men he eventually beat into second and third places overall.

Ole Olsen, three times the champion and a Wembley 'specialist', so nearly carried off the title again, at the age of thirty-four. And one of his Danish proteges, nineteen-year-old Tommy Knudsen, a fine emerging talent, was the other rider who showed his back wheel to Penhall for so long that it seemed he could not be beaten.

But each time the American, driven by the same unseen force that has carried others – Olsen included – beyond ordinary ambition and achievement, snatched the verdict on the line amid scenes of mass hysteria.

Penhall's battle with Olsen in heat seven was a true classic. Egon Muller (West Germany) and Hans Nielsen (Denmark), two very capable riders, were in the same race but I have to be honest and say I cannot remember seeing them after the first corner! All eyes were riveted on the action up front, where Olsen, as cunning as a fox, rode as if his own eyes were in the back of his head.

Wherever and whenever Penhall attacked, Olsen moved to close the gap. One moment they were up against the white line, then they were sliding wide towards the fence. On the final lap, first corner, uncannily their front wheels lifted in unison as they picked up some dirt. It was as if Penhall was Olsen's shadow.

The last turn . . . surely Olsen could not be caught. He had dictated the race, called the tune.

From my seat in the Wembley Press Box, high above the red shale track, it appeared Olsen had gone wide enough to shut off any last-gasp challenge. But he hadn't. Penhall plunged through the gap, his red helmet-cover a blur but, as they crossed the line, noticeably a foot ahead of the yellow and black of Olsen!

No one seated twenty yards either side of the finishing line could have separated them. But if that was close, Penhall's victory over Tommy Knudsen, in heat 14, was indistinguishable.

The action on the first corner was pulsating enough with Knudsen drifting wide after making the gate, then swooping back under Penhall in frightening fashion and accelerating away like an express train down the back straight. Penhall couldn't believe it as he set off in pursuit. If he was going to be world champion he had to produce another miracle. And he did.

Scrawled in my notebook, a souvenir from that memorable night, are three words, almost indecipherable because they were written at about the same speed as Penhall's bike . . . 'Penhall on line'. It was an instant judgement but we had to wait, breathlessly, for Australian referee Sam Bass to confirm that the American had done it again – and Knudsen wasn't convinced at all.

He had punched the air jubilantly himself as they slowed after the flag!

But Penhall was 12 points to the good and fate was determining that he needed only one more to be champion. His last race could have been a sensational showdown

with England's gutsy newcomer Kenny Carter, his arch rival in a long season. But Carter's marvellous world final debut disintegrated into despair when his engine failed him in heat fifteen.

In that same heat, Dave Jessup's second breakdown of the night left the redoubtable little man from King's Lynn wondering why somebody up there dislikes him so much on world final night.

Two scorching wins had put the England captain in good heart and there was no hint of a repeat of the misfortune that had wrecked his chances in Wembley's last final, three years earlier. But heat nine had been a nightmare. He had chased Penhall

to the last corner only for a jubilee clip, value 30p, to break, causing the carburettor to come adrift.

Carter, a dynamic twenty-year-old from Yorkshire, was more bewildered than disgusted when he stopped in heat 15. He had gone out on one of Ivan Mauger's bikes, a machine that had not lost a race. It did this time.

Erik Gundersen, another of the Danish World Team Cup-winning squad, overcame some heartache of his own to finish with two late wins and 11 points in his first individual final. But he was almost beyond consolation earlier when carburettor trouble caused his engine to cut out.

The twenty-one-year-old from Esjberg had taken 5 points from his first two rides and jumped into the lead in his third when disaster struck. Elated one moment, distraught the next he sat white-faced in the dressing room shedding tears of disappointment.

Bruce Penhall sat white-faced, too, between heats 14 and 20. There was too much time to think when speedway's greatest prize was only four laps away.

Ironically, by the time Penhall pulled on his goggles and helmet cover for that all-important final race, the defending champion had showered and changed! Michael Lee's controversial reign as title holder had ended ignominiously . . . with the England international on his backside.

Only a machine failure or a mind-blowing act of stupidity could have prevented Penhall from taking the title. As it was, he lost out to Carter in the race for the first turn and, apart from a token challenge, he did just enough to ensure that

15

he stayed in second spot. Then, as he rounded the pits corner for the last time, he knew the title was his and he produced a characteristic 'wheelie' to signal a start to the celebrations.

Amazing scenes followed. Everyone wanted to congratulate Penhall even before he had returned to the pits . . . friends, relations, associates, fans etc etc. His Cradley Heath team-mate Erik Gundersen swallowed his own disappointment to throw his arms around the American. There was a bear hug from his Cradley team boss Peter Adams, another from his American pals Harry Oxley and Bobby Schwartz . . . and then there was his family!

Nicknamed 'Penhall's party' these jubilant Californians thronged the pits area and filled the air with their whoops of joy. Sadly, of course, two very important people were missing, Penhall's parents, killed in a private plane crash a few years earlier. But they were not forgotten. When the new champion took the microphone after the official presentation, he told the vast crowd: 'My parents rode every race with me.'

And later, in a crowded Press interview room, he added: 'My mother never watched me race speedway but my dad said that as long as I enjoyed the sport I could carry on and he would give me all the help I wanted. So I really wanted to win the world championship for them . . . and for my brothers and sisters and everyone else who has helped and supported me.

'I came to the meeting very relaxed this year but the final race was a bit tense. I had one worry because I had to change my bike for that one. Pete Adams found traces of metal in the oil of my best bike and it could have seized up. So I went out on my No. 2 bike just in case.

'Pete was terrific. He told me "Take it easy and don't do anything stupid." I guess I looked behind a few times but I made it. I had hoped to make five starts but it didn't work out that way and I had some really hard races.

'The race with Ole was really tight and the one with Tommy Knudsen even closer.'

While the cameras whirred and flashed and Penhall coped courteously and manfully with a torrent of questions, Yorkshire's Kenny Carter reflected on his first appearance at Wembley. He looked bitterly disappointed. But Ivan Mauger, who had been at his side all night, told me: 'On his performance tonight he would have been in with a great chance but for that one engine failure. I'm very impressed with Kenny and I'm sure he will win it in the next two or three years.'

How strange it was to see Ivan in mechanic's overalls on world final night, even stranger to see him advertising the name 'Weslake' after all his years under the 'Jawa' banner! And what did it feel like to be tending to someone else's needs instead of his own?

'Different, certainly. I had to make decisions for somebody else instead of me. It was Kenny's first Wembley and I've ridden here enough times to know what is required, mechanically and riding-wise. There is more to riding in a world final than dropping the clutch and burning your way round the first turn. You need two positive strategies, one for if you make the start and another for if you don't. The important thing is that Kenny is prepared to listen.'

But Wembley 1981 was not about the past or the future. It was about the present. And for an all-American boy and 92,000 cosmopolitan fans it was a wonderful, wonderful experience.

16

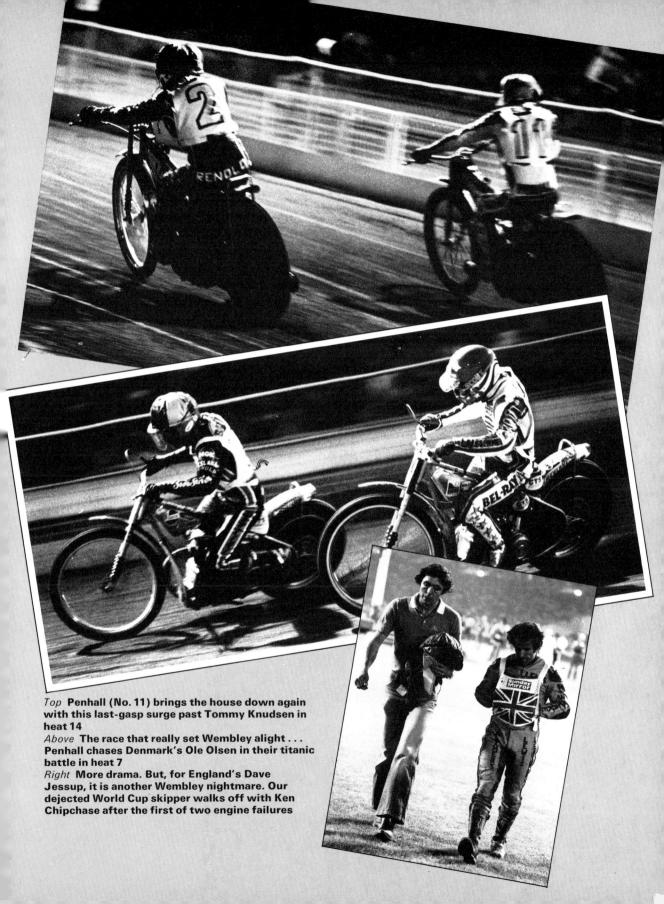

Top **Penhall (No. 11) brings the house down again with this last-gasp surge past Tommy Knudsen in heat 14**

Above **The race that really set Wembley alight . . . Penhall chases Denmark's Ole Olsen in their titanic battle in heat 7**

Right **More drama. But, for England's Dave Jessup, it is another Wembley nightmare. Our dejected World Cup skipper walks off with Ken Chipchase after the first of two engine failures**

I'm not a fake!
says world champion Bruce Penhall

I'm having a great time being world champion – but it's not all a bed of roses. Trying to be a good ambassador for the sport is hard work. Things started happening for me from the moment I won that world title at Wembley last September.

The previous year, I'd gone home to California after finishing fifth in the Gothenburg world final. I was choked. I sat around doing nothing but feel sorry for myself. This time I didn't have a spare moment when I got back to the States.

One TV talk show was fantastic. I went on the Merv Griffin Show on KT TV in Hollywood, appearing with film star Joan Collins, Beach Boys singer Mike Love and comedian Jerry Van Dyke.

Man, that show was so big. It went out to 48 million people in eleven countries. And I guess it really opened a few doors for me. . . and for speedway!

I've had a few interviews and acting classes because I want to project a good image when I go on TV. All I've ever been is a motor cycle racer. Now there's talk about me going into films and stuff and although I never thought of it before, I've got to admit it sounds exciting and interesting. My head is full of so many new ideas right now – but although I have been tempted to retire I'm not going to turn my

back on speedway just yet. That's still number one on my plate.

I've had a lot out of speedway and I want to give something back. I hope to do that by being a good champion and maybe helping the sport to expand in the States.

It could do with a boost in Britain, too, because a lot of tracks are struggling. I think people need to be entertained . . . that's why I try to do something a bit different, to leave them with a smile on their faces when they go home after a meeting.

Everybody knows I like to do a 'wheelie' when I cross the line. And I guess people would have been disappointed if I hadn't done one at Wembley after my last race. Some guys have given me stick for showing off and a couple have called me a 'big-headed so and so' but never to my face.

It doesn't bother me. It would if I had a 'fake' personality but I haven't. All I want to do is entertain the fans and make sure they come back next week. What's wrong with that? Does that make me big-headed?

When Dan McCormick first brought me to England he tried to get me to cut out the 'wheelies'. And my new team boss at

The long wait before his last race at Wembley . . . and the tension shows in Bruce Penhall's face

18

Cradley Heath, Pete Adams, doesn't like me doing them either. But it's no big deal and I certainly don't do it to show off or offend my rivals on the track, even if some of them think so.

I've got to admit I've been fined and warned by a few referees but that won't stop me from doing something that pleases most of the fans.

You can read about Wembley elsewhere in this book and what I thought about it. What a fantastic year . . . what with winning the world championship, taking the world pairs title for America with my buddy Bobby Schwartz, helping Cradley to win the British League championship and then being voted Coral-SWAPA Rider of the Year.

What impact has it had on speedway in America? It's difficult to say. But I guess the American people are starting to come alive to the fact that there is something other than baseball, American football, tennis and the rest.

Speedway is still pretty small in the States with only a few tracks. The two main ones are at Costa Mesa and San Bernardino and nearly all the good riders come from Southern California. It's hard to get them to go to other tracks because it doesn't

really pay unless you're on a good guarantee.

I hope my world championship win does give speedway a boost in the States. I'd love to see a Grand Prix circuit taking in places like Oklahoma and Texas. But the country is so big that before I won the world championship I was virtually unknown.

It's only since I appeared on that coast-to-coast TV show and other TV channels that people have got to hear they've got a world champion at speedway. And every time I appear on TV I take the opportunity to advertise the fact that we've got a world final in Los Angeles on 28 August 1982.

Only a few years ago I'd never heard of the British League or the world championship! When Scott Autrey was making his name in Britain, we kinda thought he'd just disappeared! But since Scott made the breakthrough quite a few guys have come over to British League and now we've got a very good American squad.

I'm not knocking the fact that speedway is still comparatively small in the States or suggesting I've been neglected in any way. The treatment I've received since my Wembley win has been fantastic.

When I flew back to Los Angeles soon after the world final and rode in meetings at

Penhall crowns his world championship win with a traditional 'wheelie'. Showing off? 'No, I do it to please the fans,' he says

Costa Mesa and San Bernardino, I got an unbelievable welcome. I was thrilled to receive a personal message of congratulation from President Reagan. Then there was a presentation made by California State Governor Gerry Brown. And if that wasn't enough, the Mayor of Costa Mesa declared a 'Bruce Penhall Day' on Friday 25 September!

I guess I feel more respected now than ever before in the eight years I've been riding speedway. I'm conscious of presenting a good image because motor cycle racers still tend to be looked upon as Hell's Angels with greasy finger-nails.

I'm sure that having an American world champion will help this year's final in Los Angeles, although it wasn't my intention to win it at Wembley to boost the 1982 final. If I could have won in Gothenburg the previous year, I would have done. I wanted it just as badly then.

The only thing I've ever wanted since I started riding speedway was to be world champion and I thought I had a good chance in Sweden. CBS did a TV special on the world final and followed me around a lot. But you have to learn to handle the pressures. It was my first world final and I started well enough, winning the first race. But I blew it after that and I was so dejected I was almost in tears when the TV guy interviewed me.

I think my last words in that interview were something like, 'I'll be here again next year.' I don't know whether or not the folks back home were sorry for me or what, but it seemed to make a big impact. I'm just glad I was able to keep my word.

What happens now? There are so many possibilities. It would mean a lot to me if I could win the championship again in front of my own people but I guess some of the other American guys have the same idea.

The 1981 American Championship was held at the Los Angeles Coliseum on the newly-laid track. I won the meeting so, obviously, I enjoyed it. But I can't say whether it will give me any advantage this year. Anyway, I haven't yet qualified!

I guess the track is about the size of Coventry's but with a big square corner. The first and second bends are a bit like Wembley but the third and fourth are very different and you have to turn twice. I think there will be plenty of passing.

Some people seem to think there will be more pressure on me because the final is in America. I don't see how it can be. Most of that pressure was released at Wembley. I've done what I wanted to do and I'm not setting out to win the championship as many times as Ivan Mauger. I don't intend to stay in speedway that long!

That doesn't mean I'm planning to quit just yet but I can't ride motor cycles all my life and there are other things I want to do. The acting idea really interests me.

I've taken on a guy called Jeff Immediato as my full-time Marketing Manager. Speedway takes up so much of my time that I need somebody to take care of all the other things. He's got the knowledge and experience of marketing and he just pushes me towards the things I want to do.

It's got to be the most exciting time of my life and I appreciate so much the people who have helped me along the way. I know, too, that without British League racing I could never have been world champion. So when I say that I want to be a good ambassador, a good champion and to give something back to the sport to help boost it on both sides of the Atlantic . . . I mean every word.

International portrait gallery

Speedway has become a truly international sport over the years and here are some of the famous names who have helped to put their respective nations on the map.

1 EGON MULLER (West Germany)
Born Kiel, 26 November 1948

Blond, extrovert star of the European and world long-track scene – and an international pop singer, too!

Egon has been world long-track champion three times, in 1974, 1975 and 1978. And he has raced in four world individual speedway finals, in 1976, 1977, 1980 and 1981. Nine points at Wembley last year represents his best world final performance so far.

Muller rides for Brokstedt in the West German Bundesliga (Northern section) and his spectacular riding style makes him a huge favourite wherever he goes. He was West German champion in 1979 and again in 1981.

British fans are disappointed that he has been so reluctant to perform regularly in the British League. He had a very brief spell with Coatbridge in 1973 and a longer one with Hull Lada Vikings in 1976.

However, he has proved himself no mean performer in top level speedway and was in great form in the 1981 World Team Cup final at Olching. Could it be that Egon will give West Germany a world champion for the first time at Norden in 1983?

2 JIRI STANCL (Czechoslovakia)
Born Zatci, 18 November 1949

Jiri belongs to the Red Star Club of Prague and is by far the most outstanding rider to come out of Czechoslovakia in modern times. He has won the national championship no fewer than *eleven* times and is the current holder.

Jiri has appeared in six world speedway individual finals and seven long-track finals. But his limited British League experience has been a handicap and his best world final performance, six points, was achieved at Katowice in 1976.

Started riding at international level in 1969 and won his first national title a year later. Since then the Prague policeman has dominated the Czech scene. But it was not until 1976 that he made his bow in the British League.

Rode for Coventry again during the 1978 season and was with Reading Racers in 1979 and 1980. Was unable to compete in the British League last season because of a ban on all Czech riders competing in England – but he is back this year.

1

2

3

4

3 ZENON PLECH (Poland)
Born Zwierzyn, 1 January 1953

Outstanding world-travelled international star who finished runner-up to Ivan Mauger in the 1979 World final in Katowice – his best performance in seven appearances.

That display in 1979 was all the more creditable because Plech, former 'boy wonder' of Polish speedway, had suffered from a heart complaint the previous year!

Zenon joined his local club Stal Gorzow at the age of sixteen and in 1972, when he was nineteen, became the youngest ever Polish national champion. A year later, in Katowice, he made a brilliant world final debut, scoring 12 points and finishing third. But he was overshadowed by the now-forgotten Jerzy Szczakiel, who stunned the world-record crowd of 130,000 by winning the title for Poland.

While Szczakiel faded, Plech became firmly established as a top-ranking international star. He toured Australia, New Zealand and America as a member of the world champions' troupe and joined Hackney Hawks in the British League, in 1975. Apart from 1977 and 1978, he has ridden for Hackney ever since.

In view of the political situation in Poland where he now rides for Gdansk, there was some doubt whether he would be able to rejoin Hackney in 1982.

4 LARRY ROSS (New Zealand)
Born Christchurch, 15 June 1954

Former moto-cross rider who won the New Zealand South Island 125cc and 250cc championships before turning his attention to speedway in 1972. That was in his home town of Christchurch, a veritable breeding ground of world champions. Ronnie Moore, Barry Briggs and Ivan Mauger are all from Christchurch and Larry hopes to follow in their footsteps by lifting the world crown.

He was non-riding reserve at Gothenburg in 1980 but made his debut at Wembley last year. Unfortunately, he managed only four points and was excluded for tape-breaking in one ride. But he did have the satisfaction of winning a race in his first world final.

Made his international debut for New Zealand in 1974, against Poland, and came to England the following season to join Wimbledon Dons. His big moment was in helping New Zealand to their first-ever World Team Cup title at White City, London, in September 1979.

New Zealand champion five years in a row, from 1976 to 1980, Larry lost out to Ivan Mauger in '81 and Mitch Shirra in '82. Transferred from Wimbledon to Belle Vue for £18,000 in 1981, to replace Peter Collins.

MIKE FERREIRA (Zimbabwe)
Born Salisbury, 21 November 1955

Began his British speedway career with Coatbridge in 1974, two years after his competitive debut in the sport at Salisbury. Returned to Rhodesia to serve in the army and did not resume his British career until 1978 when he linked up with Canterbury in the National League.

Mike also made three British League appearances for Exeter Falcons in the 1978 season. Took over as Canterbury's No. 1 in 1979, averaging 8.53, and continued to improve in 1980. But last season was the big one and he achieved his last ambition at National League level by winning the Riders' Championship at Wimbledon.

He started favourite, despite a ligament injury, and looked 'different class' as he romped to a 15-points maximum.

Now he is determined to make his mark in the British League with Swindon Robins, the team he joined last season.

FINN THOMSEN (Denmark)
Born Arhus, 16 February 1955

Another former moto-cross rider who first made his mark with the Arhus Motor Club in Denmark before becoming Danish Junior Champion in 1973. The following year he rode in the World Pairs Championship as partner to Ole Olsen and was runner-up in the Danish Senior Championship.

That same year, Finn came to Britain and joined Wolverhampton, with whom he spent four seasons. In his last year at Monmore Green, he made his world final debut in Sweden. And what an impressive performance! He scored ten points on a rain-sodden track to finish in fifth place.

Finn quit Wolverhampton and joined Hackney Hawks for the 1978 season. He had a comparatively mediocre year with the Hawks but firmly established himself at international level, helping Denmark to win the World Team Cup for the first time and finishing third with Olsen in the Pairs final.

In 1979 he reached his second world final, in Poland, but could manage only six points – disappointing after coming third in the Inter-continental final.

In 1980, Finn qualified for his third world final, in Gothenburg, but was well down the field again.

He was reserve for Denmark when they regained the World Team Cup in Olching last season but made an early exit from the individual championship. Ended the year by helping Bruce Penhall's World Select to win the Lada Indoor International at Wembley Arena.

STEVE BASTABLE (England)
Born Birmingham, 16 September 1956

Son of former Cradley Heath skipper and England international Harry Bastable and, understandably, began his career at Dudley Wood – by practising after the meetings when he was a fifteen-year-old!

Began his league racing career in 1974 when he made thirty-three appearances for Stoke in the Second Division and ten for Cradley in the First. Steve was runner-up in the British Junior Championship the same year.

He settled down to become a valuable

member of the Cradley outfit and was very much a part of the big revival under flamboyant promoter Dan McCormick. But then came trouble. After returning to the track after an ankle injury, Steve had a bust-up with his promoter and was transferred to Birmingham. That was in September 1979.

The following season, with Steve now installed as skipper at Perry Barr, Dan McCormick suddenly arrived on the scene. No problems, initially, and Steve had a moderately successful season and also reached the semi-finals of the World Long-track championship at the first attempt.

But during the 1980–81 close season he learned that Birmingham didn't want him any more and he was seriously considering quitting the sport for good.

And what a disaster that would have been! Fortunately offers came in from Belle Vue and Swindon and Steve opted for a move to Blunsdon. A few months later, in June 1981, he was crowned British Champion at Coventry!

DENNIS SIGALOS (USA)

Born Garden Grove, California,
16 August 1959

Flamboyant American who has made a tremendous impact since arriving in Britain only a few years ago. Joined Hull Lada Vikings in 1979 and soon became a firm favourite on Humberside.

But after an even more successful season, in 1980, he moved to Ipswich Witches for a world record transfer fee estimated at £30,000. The deal also involved Australian Billy Sanders, who moved to Hull, and Sigalos's fellow American John Cook who was transferred to Ipswich.

Sigalos began riding speedway bikes when he was thirteen, at the Orange County Raceway, Los Angeles. He became America's top mini-speedway rider.

In 1980 he established himself at top level by winning the *Daily Mirror*-Berger Grand Prix and helped America to beat England in the Test series. Rode for America in the World Team Cup final in Wroclaw.

After linking up with Ipswich last season he finished second in the American final of the 1981 World Championship and followed that with 10 points in the Overseas final at White City.

However, he helped Ipswich to win the *Speedway Star* Knock-out Cup and there is no doubt he has the ability to beat the best in the world on his day.

VLADIMIR GORDEEV (Russia)
Born May, Georgia, 30 November 1950

Outstanding Soviet rider of the seventies with only one blot on his record. Finished fourth in the 1971 world final in Sweden but was disqualified and later banned following a fuel test which revealed an additive in his fuel.

This apart no one can deny that Vladimir, the elder of two brothers from the Balakovo Club, has a magnificent record at top level.

A former metal worker, he began his career in 1968 and within a year made his international debut, against Poland. Also in 1970, he reached the world final in Wroclaw, scoring five points.

Soviet junior champion in 1968 he has won the senior national title on four occasions, in 1971, 1973, 1974 and 1978. One of the highlights of his career was winning the Continental final in 1974.

His younger brother Valeri was Soviet champion in 1975 and 1977. He also rides for the Balakovo Club.

PHIL CRUMP (Australia)
Born Mildura, Victoria, 9 February 1952

Phil ended Australia's long years in the world championship wilderness by finishing third in the 1976 world individual final in Poland and leading his country to their first and only triumph in the World Team Cup that same year.

Now established with Swindon Robins, he first came to prominence in England in 1971 with Crewe and the following year won the Second Division Riders' championship. Only two years later he won the first of his Australian titles and finished third in the British League Riders' championship, representing Newport.

Phil moved on to Bristol in 1977 but they closed after two seasons and he was switched to Swindon. Missed most of the 1980 season because of business commitments back in Australia. Made no impression in last year's world championship because he didn't get past the Australasian final.

The grand slump
by Richard Bott

The hard, cold facts are that after the GRAND SLAM came the GRAND SLUMP. England's speedway riders ruled the world in 1980 . . . team, pairs and individual champions. Success was built by and around six men: **Ian Thomas** (Team Manager), **Eric Boocock** (Team Coach) and four great riders **Michael Lee**, **Peter Collins**, **Dave Jessup** and **Chris Morton**.

But when England began the defence of the first-ever triple crown, they did so without fifty per cent of that formidable squad.

Ian Thomas had been unable to continue as team manager, for health reasons; Eric Boocock had resigned because of pressure of work; Peter Collins had retired from British Speedway and was considered ineligible for selection, though a bad arm injury would have reduced his effectiveness, anyway.

So we started the 1981 season with a new team manager, Hackney's effervescent promoter **Len Silver**, and a new team captain, King's Lynn flyer **Dave Jessup**.

And we started it superbly! So did the much-maligned Len Silver! The only blemish on England's record the previous year had been a Test series defeat (3–1 with one drawn) by America. Revenge was sweet when England stormed to a 4–1 victory early in 1981.

THE WAR OF WORDS HAD ALREADY BEGUN. A DELIGHTED LEN SILVER SAID: 'ENGLAND'S ACHIEVEMENTS OF LAST YEAR HAVE BEEN RAMMED DOWN MY THROAT. BUT WE DIDN'T BEAT AMERICA LAST YEAR. NOW WE HAVE.'

Victory was the only pleasure to be gleaned from the first Test raced in almost sub-zero temperature at Belle Vue on Sunday 26 April. Driving sleet and biting wind made life very uncomfortable for riders, mechanics and 4000 shivering fans – less than half the expected attendance.

It was strange to see an England team without Peter Collins but the family tradition was upheld by the inclusion of his brothers Les and Phil, who contributed to a 60–48 win. And new skipper Dave Jessup, riding a Godden for the first time, was voted *Daily Mirror* Man of the Match.

Down on the south coast three days later, Poole was the venue for a thrill-a-minute second Test in much more agreeable conditions. The match see-sawed with America twice in front by six points. But England came up with a trump card on the

The writing was on the wall for England as early as the Inter-continental final at King's Lynn. But America fared even worse. Our picture shows a disconsolate Kelly Moran and Bruce Penhall after America had failed to qualify for the final

night, reserve rider Gordon Kennett. The Eastbourne Eagle top-scored with 12 points and was Man of the Match, as England scraped home 55–53. Tough on the Yanks . . . particularly Dennis Sigalos (15 points) and Bruce Penhall (14) who were both in brilliant form.

England now had the bit between their teeth and they took a winning 3–0 lead in the series when they triumphed 64–43 at Swindon on 2 May. And it was a triumph because, after four heats, we were trailing by *12 points*! Michael Lee was in tremendous form, reeling off five wins after a third place first time out.

Was it going to be a whitewash? Not if Bruce Penhall and Co could help it. And they could. There was no disputing their determination at Ipswich, where Dennis Sigalos and John Cook had home-track advantage. Unfortunately, a marvellous match was cut short by a downpour.

America led by four points going into heat 16 . . . then the rain came down in torrents. Cook and Penhall raced through the rain to record a 5–1 over Kennett and Lee and that was where it ended. Referee Graham Brodie had no alternative but to abandon the meeting with two heats left and America leading 52–44.

The result was allowed to stand but would it have been, I wonder, if the series had depended on the result?

Anyway, if Ipswich boosted America's morale, Cradley, on 10 May, shattered it again. Penhall, on the track where he is so revered, had a disastrous night, falling in two of his rides, and Dennis Sigalos was a huge disappointment, scoring one point.

England, spearheaded by skipper Jessup (17), ran up their highest score of the series. They were 18 points ahead halfway through and won in a canter, 69–38. Result of the series: England 4, USA 1.

A week later, at Reading, England began their defence of the World Team Cup and splashed their way to victory in the United Kingdom qualifying round. With Gordon Kennett replacing Peter Collins from the quartet which won the trophy in Poland the previous year, England won a rain-affected meeting with 36 points to America's 32. But, really, it was all about qualifying for the Inter-continental Final and there was no pressure on the reigning champions since Australia (20) and New Zealand (8) had little to offer.

So what happened to the Grand Slump? England, represented by Chris Morton and Dave Jessup, had qualified for the World Pairs final in Poland on 20 June. They had finished level, on 23 points, with New Zealand and West Germany in the semi-final at Norden. There was no reason to suspect that they would not acquit themselves well in the final against the Kiwis and the Germans plus host nation Poland and the three qualifiers from the other semi-final . . . Denmark, America and Czechoslovakia.

The Test series against the Danes had got underway on 12 June, with a 62–46 win on

Len Silver's Hackney track and Jessup had been in blistering form.

But our world came crashing down in Katowice when America's Bruce Penhall and Bobby Schwartz, the inseparable Californian kids, took the Pairs title in style and *England finished joint fifth!*

What a shaker! It was not until heat ten that Jessup and Morton got it together with a 5–1 and that was against two Polish reserves! The West German pair, Egon Muller and Georg Gilgenreiner, had crashed in heat seven and, though not seriously hurt, withdrawn from the meeting.

Penhall and Schwartz pipped New Zealand's Ivan Mauger and Larry Ross by one point to give America a world title for

the first time in forty-four years. And their victory would have been more emphatic if Penhall's machine had not stopped when he was a clear leader in his second ride.

America totalled 23 points, New Zealand 22 and third place went to the hard-riding Poles (Zenon Plech and Eddie Jancarz) with 21 points. Plech gave the 70,000 crowd plenty to shout about by accumulating 15 points.

In fact, the Poles could have forced a run-off with Penhall and Schwartz. They went into the twenty-first and final heat needing a 5–1 over Denmark to tie for first place. But Hans Nielsen, with only four points to his name, denied the home duo with his first win of the afternoon.

Czechoslovakia were the surprise packets, nipping into fourth place (18 points) ahead of England and Denmark (17 each). West Germany brought up the rear with three points but only completed one race.

So it was a sad day for England after the euphoria of the previous year when Jessup and Collins had piled up 29 points in Yugoslavia. Jessup was the subject of a random drug test after the Katowice meeting. It was negative, of course. But perhaps the Poles couldn't believe the little man could have such an off day!

With no hope of achieving the Grand Slam again England turned their attention to the World Team Cup and what a fight they had to put up before they squeezed through to the final.

The Inter-continental round at King's Lynn was a hell-raiser. Sweden were no-hopers but champions England found the Danes and the Americans a real double handful. With four heats left we were on the way out, in third spot. But Dave Jessup stormed to his only win of the afternoon in heat thirteen, and British champion Steve Bastable, who had come into the line-up in place of Gordon Kennett, fought his way to the front in the next race.

So we made it to the final in Olching but Denmark's performance at King's Lynn was a warning bell ringing loudly in every Englishman's ear.

It must be said that the staging of a Test match in Denmark only two days before the King's Lynn meeting was hardly the ideal preparation for such an important World Cup event . . . for either side. England lost that friendly 60–48 at Vojens but went on to win the Test series.

Action from the final in Olching . . . Denmark's Hans Nielsen (*left*) battles with England's John Davis

Four of our five hopefuls for the individual championship survived a farcical Inter-continental final at Vojens on 25 July. John Louis, enjoying a new lease of life after his move from Ipswich to Halifax, was the only Englishman to fall by the wayside on a sodden track more suited to ducks than dirt-track racing. More of that later.

World champion Mike Lee, for all his troubles, did enough to qualify for Wembley along with Kenny Carter, Chris Morton and Dave Jessup. But Bruce Penhall's victory, in atrocious conditions, sounded another warning.

Next on the world championship calendar, however, was the World Team Cup final, the meeting which provoked the greatest controversy of all as far as England's fall from grace was concerned.

Len Silver did not attend the practice in Olching and Michael Lee declared himself unfit to ride. John Davis took his place even though Gordon Kennett had already been named as reserve.

We didn't win, we didn't ever look like winning. It was Denmark's day from the moment Dave Jessup's engine failed in the first heat. Chris Morton rode his heart out on the sun-baked track but England were not good enough to hang on to their title and that was the overriding factor even though their morale had been undermined by the events of the previous day.

Denmark's winning margin was seven points and England squeezed into second spot a point ahead of the West Germans, the Soviet Union looking desperately outclassed though their inadequate machinery gave them no chance.

So the Grand Slump was almost complete. England had lost two world titles and the third was to go at Wembley three weeks later.

It may well be that too much credit was given to Ian Thomas and Eric Boocock when England achieved the Grand Slam and that too much blame was laid at the feet of Len Silver when a golden year was followed by the Grand Slump.

But every England team manager, whether it be speedway, football, cricket, tennis or tiddly-winks, must know that he will be judged by results.

I doubt whether Len Silver would have been given any credit if an English rider had won the 1981 World Championship.

Ironically, Len Silver's preparation of the Wembley track, which was above reproach, indirectly helped Bruce Penhall to 'steal' England's last crown. Had the track not been conducive to good racing, Penhall might never have produced those two cliffhanger wins.

And there is even greater irony in the fact that Len Silver's unstinting work at Wembley was, in the eyes of many, his undoing as England team manager.

The critics

Team Manager **Len Silver** took the brunt of the criticism for England's failure to win a world speedway title in 1981. At the end of the day he found he had few friends among his fellow promoters, the riders or the media.

But not all the criticism was levelled at one man. **Philip Rising**, editor of *Speedway Star* and secretary of the Speedway Writers and Photographers' Association, was far more sweeping in his condemnation of England's lack of success.

Philip Rising (Editor of *Speedway Star***) speaks out during the controversial England debate at the first British Speedway Supporters' Convention in Blackpool. On the panel, (***left to right***) are: Peter Collins, John Berry, Eric Boocock, Ian Thomas, Philip Rising, Len Silver and Michael Lee**

England missed the skill and experience of Peter Collins when he took a year off from British speedway. He is pictured watching the British final, at Coventry, with Cradley promoter Peter Adams

In the *Speedway Star* on 22 August 1981 he wrote:

'English speedway needs to take a long, hard look at itself after the World Team Cup eclipse in Bavaria on Sunday.

'The loss of the World Pairs crown and the team trophy is a clear indication that while the riders have tried and done their best, something is wrong. A number of questions have to be asked and some vital decisions taken . . . and the sooner the better.

'The lack of organization for the England team in Olching was astonishing and as long as this penny-saving, amateurish attitude remains, our performances in the international arena will not improve.

'This is not the time to point the finger at individuals but those who hold the collective responsibility should examine their own consciences.

'England arrived in West Germany without a team manager and in a state of chaos that should never have been allowed. The riders were expected to organize the transportation of their own bikes to Olching, even to provide the funds for the petrol en route – although this was reimbursed later – and to sort themselves out at the vitally important practice session.

'At one stage, the organizers told the riders they couldn't practise without body colours, which they didn't have at that

Eric Boocock, who helped England to achieve the Grand Slam in 1980, is back in charge. Here he talks tactics with two of his Belle Vue riders, Jim McMillan and Keith Bloxsome

moment . . . and Dave Jessup is sure he wasn't given his full time on the track.

'These are not excuses for England's defeat against an exceptional Danish team. But the team spirit which was established last year, and which undoubtedly helped win the pairs and team cups, has been allowed to slip away.

'It was left to unofficial helpers to do what they could but if speedway wants to be considered as a major sport, which it is, then the governing bodies must start to act accordingly.

'The job of England team manager must go to someone who is prepared to give it the time and energy it requires. If that means looking outside the realms of the British

promoters, all of whom have their priorities with their own tracks, then so be it.

'After all, why should the manager be a promoter? And the events of the past two months have proved that whoever is given the job must have an experienced and capable assistant.

'It is a two-man job, at least, and while the promoters will claim that there isn't the money in speedway to justify a full-time appointment, some remuneration must be paid.

'It is time British speedway moved into the eighties instead of stumbling along making a hash of giving the national team the lift and backing it deserves . . . .

'There is too much passing the buck and

if the BSPA are not prepared to make the necessary appointments then the Control Board should step in . . . .

'Attitudes are important and it is not enough to simply cast aside defeats in the pairs and team competitions as being unimportant. Members of the BSPA are, essentially, businessmen and some lack the sporting instincts that motivate the riders, the fans and the Press.

'It is easy to be proud when England win but there is not enough remorse and soul-searching when things go wrong, as they have done this year.

'The BSPA should immediately set up a committee, including Dave Jessup and Chris Morton and representatives from both the SCB and themselves, to ensure that England lead the world on and off the track. BUT WILL IT HAPPEN?'

THIS IS WHAT THE RIDERS SAID:

CHRIS MORTON The World Team Cup final in Olching was like an ordinary open meeting. It should be something special when you ride for England. The lack of organization didn't affect my performance but it could have affected the others.

I think it's time to speak out now in the hope that something will be done . . . otherwise I shall have to consider whether I want to ride for England next year!

MICHAEL LEE I missed the World Team Cup final through illness but we were not working as a team leading up to the final. This was partly to do with Peter Collins being out of the team. I think everyone was a bit lost when he dropped out. After all, he had been captain the previous year.

There was bad organization and everybody knows it. We've got to hope it won't happen in the future. Personally, I think the two-man set-up of 1980 was the best.

PETER COLLINS (England's captain when they achieved the Grand Slam but ruled ineligible to ride in 1981 because he had retired from British League racing): As an outsider this season but having talked to the other riders, they felt they were not a team!

It's all down to motivation and confidence and this was lacking.

IAN THOMAS AND ERIC BOOCOCK WERE ENGLAND'S MANAGEMENT TEAM IN THE SUCCESSFUL GRAND SLAM SEASON. WHAT DID THEY THINK?

IAN THOMAS (Hull and Newcastle promoter who was team manager in 1980 but had to relinquish the job for health reasons): Personally I would criticize the BSPA because they gave Len Silver too much to do. There is no way any man can operate Hackney and Rye House, prepare the Wembley track – that's a hell of a job and it was a credit to speedway and Len Silver in particular – and devote the necessary time to running the England team.

Eric Boocock and I probably took more stick than Len Silver . . . from the Press over our selections, and from the BSPA because we wanted to do things our way. But there was no question of compromise and there shouldn't be.

ERIC BOOCOCK (England's coach in 1980, he resigned after the Grand Slam but has since taken over from Len Silver as team manager for 1982): You've got to do the job your own way because you are judged on results. If you win you're great, if you lose you're rubbish.

It's important that you look like a team and act like a team and I don't think England did in 1981.

Silver's Lining

Len Silver *is fifty years old and has been a promoter since he retired from riding in 1964 after a distinguished career. A Londoner, he won the Provincial League Riders' Championship in 1962. Promoter at Hackney and Rye House, he became England team manager for the second time in 1981. Six years earlier, in West Germany, he had stood on the rostrum after England's World Team Cup triumph. And it was to West Germany that England travelled for the 1981 final – as* defending champions. This time there was no glory, no hour of triumph. England were outclassed by the dashing Danes and early-season victories over the USA and Denmark were forgotten as Len Silver was made the scapegoat.

How much was he to blame? Did the Press crucify him? Did the riders let him down? The arguments rage on. But now that you have read the accusations and met some of the accusers, **Len Silver** *has his say . . . .*

England's line-up for the World Team Cup final in West Germany. Left to right: Gordon Kennett, John Davis, Kenny Carter, Chris Morton, skipper Dave Jessup and team manager Len Silver

I wonder what criticism there would have been, if any, had England won the World Team Cup. It wouldn't have been, 'Where were the body colours on practice day?' or, 'There was no organization.' It would have been, 'Good old England, we've done it again!'

What did we face at Olching? I'll tell you. The strongest Danish team there has ever been. There were no other runners in the competition apart from ourselves, no one else to take points off the Danes. And we faced that situation without arguably the two best English riders of all time . . . Peter Collins and Michael Lee.

One was missing because he was not riding in the British League – and was semi-injured – and the other was ill.

I believe that *no team manager* would have been necessary for England to win that meeting in Olching *if* those two riders, on normal form, had been there.

We lost by seven points, six for mechanical problems. You could say we lost four points in heat one alone, three we would have had for winning because Dave Jessup was leading when his engine stopped . . . and the extra point the Danes picked up as a result!

In another race, John Davis stopped when he was lying second.

I'll tell you why we lost the World Cup. Not because of bad organization . . . that is utter rubbish. We lost because we didn't have Michael Lee there, because we didn't have Peter Collins there . . . because we didn't have the best team on the day!

I have been criticized for not attending the practice before the final and for bad organization. Let's take the 'bad organization' first. After we qualified for the final, several weeks before the meeting in Olching, I spoke to Dave Jessup, the England captain, and asked him how the riders wanted to travel. He said not to make any decision then because the commitments of the riders were not known.

Wilmslow World Travel, who sponsor Chris Morton, then came forward and offered to reserve flight tickets and to look after all the hotel arrangements. This offer was accepted. I got in touch with one of our sponsors at Hackney to supply a van to take the bikes across by sea. Dave Jessup's mechanic was scheduled to take charge of that job.

All the riders, except one, travelled on a flight to Munich together. The machines went out together and everything was properly organized.

Next we come to the practice . . . and there is a very good reason why I was not there for it. I wanted to be there – *not* that I regard attending practice as important as some of the riders seem to do by their comments. And I feel they have been geed up to make them.

It is a well-known fact that many top-class English riders don't like attending practice and, in some cases, don't. But let's accept that they did on this occasion.

The World Team Cup final took place in mid-August at a time when I had a dual role to fill. I was responsible for putting in the track for the World Individual Championship final at Wembley. Now that is not a job I would consider delegating to twenty workmen. I, physically, get hold of the shovel and do the job myself.

It wasn't all gloom for the much-maligned Len Silver. He waves to the crowd after England had clinched the Test series against America. BSPA chairman Wally Mawdsley is on the extreme left of the back row and the riders are Malcolm Simmons, Dave Jessup, Chris Morton and Michael Lee. Front row: John Davis, Steve Bastable, Les Collins and Gordon Kennett

Let me say, at this point, that I never felt that I couldn't do the Wembley track and be England manager. As far as I'm concerned the jobs didn't conflict – except on this one occasion. And I've told you why we lost at Olching – *not* because I missed the practice.

Now here is my schedule for the day of the practice at Olching. It was a Friday morning and I was at Wembley Stadium by 7a.m. I worked on the track all day because it was the last available day to put the finishing touches to all the base work. That's because the famous Wembley turf was being put back the following day in readiness for the FA Charity Shield football match a week later.

I worked at Wembley until about 4.30 p.m. and then hurried across to Hackney where my team had quite an important British League match against Cradley Heath. I left Hackney during the interval of the match and drove to Dover where I was booked on the 11.30 p.m. ferry. But there was such a queue of holiday traffic that I did not get into the dock until 11.35 and missed the ferry.

I was placed in the queue for the 2.30 a.m. ferry but, although I did not realize it at the time, I had been put in the wrong queue. The ferry was almost fully loaded before I realized what had happened and my determination to get on to that ferry resulted in me being summoned to appear before Dover magistrates for reckless driving!

The ferry arrived at Zeebrugge, in Belgium, at about 6.30 on Saturday morning and, anxious to be with the England team as soon as possible, I drove non-stop to Munich, arriving at about 4.30 in the afternoon. There I found all the

riders ensconced in the proper hotel, as organized by the travel agent, and all the members of the Control Board and various other members of the BSPA sipping glasses of champagne . . . which was very pleasant!

Somebody then asked me, 'Where were the body colours for the practice?' I said they were not essential for the practice and that they were in my car ready for the event the next day.

Chris Morton is one of the riders who has complained about the bad organization for the final. I didn't notice any complaint from him about the travelling arrangements for the World Pairs final in Poland when it suited him to travel independently because he had a private booking in Germany!

Another thing. All of the England riders in the World Team Cup final squad earned something approaching £100 each as an absolute bonus on the travel arrangements, because the official allowance was X and it only cost us Y and they pocketed the difference. And I don't remember them complaining about that!

The position of England team manager is not one I have ever sought. I have been manager twice and each time I was invited to take the job.

On this occasion, I took the job on the strict understanding that:

1 I would not be responsible for team selection. I felt this was a job for the BSPA management committee
2 I would not be involved in making travelling arrangements or organizing body colours or seeing to the welfare of the riders
3 I would be team manager . . . the man who made the decisions *on the day*, who spoke to the riders in the dressing rooms and engendered team spirit.

But, despite this, the job of organizing transport etc was thrust upon me, even though I did not consider it to be part of the original job.

As you know, the England job came up for begging at the start of the season. Ian Thomas was sick and Eric Boocock didn't want the position. In fact, *nobody wanted it*. And I've got to say that it's a thankless job.

Why did I take it? The chairman of the BSPA, Wally Mawdsley, rang me up and said, 'We're in trouble . . . will you do it?' I'd had a certain amount of success before and, to be honest, the job does have certain compensations. It gives the manager a voice in the Press and the publicity can be of some benefit to his own track.

But you learn, when you are in the public eye, that you are a hero one minute and a villain the next. What you do not expect is a fickle reaction from your fellow promoters. I feel that last season some of them let the position of England team manager down rather badly.

I have resigned for that reason. The criticism from my colleagues in the BSPA was very unjust.

I accept that the public, who pay their money, have the right to praise and criticize. They do not know of the problems behind the scenes. Yet my fellow promoters, who do know all the facts, forgot the victories over America and Denmark and thought only of the result of the World Team Cup in Olching.

If England fail to qualify for the World Team Cup final at White City this year, I hate to think what their reaction will be.

That is why I suggested the responsibility be shared for the all-important Inter-continental stage at Vojens, when England, Denmark and America meet with only two final places to be won.

The trouble with British speedway

Ivan Mauger, MBE (New Zealand), *Six-times World Champion and winner of every honour in the sport, has never been afraid to speak his mind. And here he takes a critical and controversial look at the current state of speedway in Britain, where he has established his own name and reputation over the past twenty-five years.*

Ivan Mauger . . . with some harsh words to say about the state of British speedway

British speedway may go bust unless the promoters stop paying riders money they can't afford . . . and unless some riders stop asking for so much cash when they don't give enough in return!

I can hear the cries of 'hypocrite' because I have always had a reputation for asking for big guarantees, signing-on fees and start money. I don't deny it. What I will say, in my defence, is that I won the World Championship before I asked for an extra penny!

Until I won the world title for the first time, in 1968, I had no sponsors, my bikes were bought and paid for by myself and, apart from the fares for my wife and family to come over from New Zealand – by sea, not by air! – I had received nothing over and above the normal rates of pay.

I maintain that I've never asked for anything I didn't figure I was worth. In fact, I reckon I must rate as THE CHEAPEST WORLD CHAMPION OF ALL TIME!

I know what about 30 per cent of the world's top riders are earning. I know the deals they have got with their respective promoters and, in some cases, I can't believe the promoters are paying that kind of cash!

I don't blame any rider for asking for as much money as he can get but a lot of them are totally unrealistic in their demands.

I can hear the promoters saying, 'He's a good one to talk!' One of them dropped the telephone last season when I told him how much I wanted to ride in an open meeting at his track. But I'll come to that in a minute.

I said earlier I was the cheapest world champion of all time. I justify that remark by saying that I know how much riders like Peter Collins and Michael Lee are asking after winning the title once. I've won it six times but I don't ask for six times as much money as they do!

41

Every promoter is complaining about his crowds being down and costs being up, yet some of them go on paying out and, unless they stop, TRACKS WILL CLOSE!

Riders and fans have a lot to be grateful for because many promoters are working on a very small profit margin, if any, and it is only their enthusiasm for the sport that keeps them and their tracks going.

Having said that, I know a hell of a lot of riders who only keep going because they love the sport. This may sound far-fetched but I'll wager that if the promoters got together today and decided to demand that the riders took a FIFTY PER CENT PAY CUT, a lot of riders would settle for that rather than give up racing.

The recession isn't solely to blame for the cash crisis in speedway. When the British League started up, in 1965, there was a tremendous amount of enthusiasm and comradeship. But things have changed for the worse.

In the last four or five years promoters have grouped together, hating other groups or individuals with a passion. They all want to put one over on the next man. I know some guys who wake up in the morning and if they haven't pulled a stroke on somebody by 9 a.m., they think it's going to be a bad day!

This attitude, unfortunately, is rubbing off on some of the riders. If you ride for Bill Smith and you've got a booking at Tom Brown's track you're supposed to do so and so.

It saddens me that there is not as much comradeship among the riders, either. One of the main reasons for this is an increasingly modern world and improved standards of living.

In the sixties we all had old cars, there were hardly any motorways and we stopped at some little cafe on one of the 'A' roads for sausage, egg and chips on the way home. So if you ran over another rider's foot during a meeting, or a fan scratched your car, by the time you'd driven twenty miles down the road and sorted it all out over a cup of tea, everyone was having a laugh again.

Nowadays, if you have a run-in with a rider, promoter or fan, you get into your nice modern motor car, get onto the nice straight modern motorway and you're home in a few hours. You may not see those guys again for a week or two so you bottle up the bad feeling.

You might argue that world champions weren't the kind of people to stop for a chat in a roadside cafe but Barry Briggs and I won most of the championships around that time and we stopped. I know I did and I've had more run-ins with people than anybody.

Speedway is a tough, competitive sport and if you intend to succeed at it you are going to have a few brushes with people on the track and exchange a few words in the pits. But so often, in those days, you got it all out of your system before you got home.

The way things have changed in the last few years, too many riders hold a grudge or are forced to carry out a vendetta on behalf of their promoter.

And the lack of comradeship among promoters contributes to the cash crisis. I'll give you a good example, without naming names.

One particular Australian rider, who is an international but is never going to make a team any better in terms of leadership or motivation, was asking a hell of a lot of money from his promoter a few years ago. And he said he wanted a transfer if he didn't get it.

Ivan Mauger, in the uncharacteristic attire of a mechanic, congratulates Bruce Penhall on his world title triumph

The promoters, at one of the council meetings, made a pact that they would not allow the rider to hold them to ransom. Yet two promoters came out of that meeting, telephoned the rider and offered him double the amount he had asked from his own promoter!

And that rider moved to one of the tracks that had offered him twice as much money. Not only that, he told some of his Australian pals what he was being paid and they started demanding more.

Not enough of today's riders are honest enough to ask themselves, 'Am I going to put x number of people on the gate?' or,

'Am I going to score enough points to justify the money I am asking?' A lot of them just think of a figure, think it sounds good and ask for it.

I DO ASK FOR A LOT OF MONEY. I make no bones about it. And I admit that, since I moved from Belle Vue to Exeter in 1973, I have had a guarantee for League matches as well as open meetings. But, until the last couple of years, I've also had an 11 point average and I can think of very few occasions when I didn't reach the second-half final and ride in it. So I reckon I've given a good return for the money. Can some others say the same?

**Close-up of a
six-times world champion**

I've always asked myself, 'Is it a fair business proposition?' before riding somewhere or asking for a guarantee. And I'm very proud of the fact that I have raced in twenty-six countries and have never been anywhere and not been asked to go back. They may not have been able to afford to have me back, but I have been asked.

As you get older you want to do less meetings. I've been used to doing well over 100 meetings a year and it was up to 160 one season. Now I'm slowing down. But it amazes me that guys of 24 and 25 are exhausted after doing seventy or eighty meetings these days. They've got it so easy . . . fast modern cars, jet aeroplanes, slick tracks you can ride with your hand tied behind your back, motorways to get them home in an hour or two . . .

Go back a few years and we were riding spindly-framed JAPs on rough, deep tracks. There were no motorways and if you went overseas it was by boat or in some rattling turbo-prop plane.

I owe plenty to speedway, make no mistake. But I've put plenty into the sport, too. A lot of business opportunities have been presented to me because I have been world champion so often and if my attitude had been totally mercenary, as some believe, I would have quit five years ago. I could have made more money outside speedway, I'm sure of that.

But I wanted to carry on being a speedway rider and the crazy thing is . . . I still do.

Face to face

Has there ever been a more controversial world champion than England's **Michael Lee?** *After the glory of Gothenburg, in September 1980, came the nightmare of 1981 . . . a diary of disaster until his surprising and sensational victory in the World Long-track Championship in Yugoslavia. The ultra-talented King's Lynn rider became the first Englishman to triumph on the long track.*

But was that adequate compensation for losing his speedway crown, for the drugs and driving convictions that rocked the sport, for the ill health that affected his form and fitness, for the clashes with authority including his own promoter, for all the unsavoury publicity?

Here are a few of the dates that Michael Lee will not care to remember from the 1981 season . . .

Michael Lee answers some leading questions from Richard Bott after his controversial year as world champion

April 16 World Champion Lee missed *Daily Express* Spring Classic. His absence upset sponsors and ITV.

June 7 Failed to turn up at Eastbourne for second leg of Golden Helmet defence against Gordon Kennett. Reported to have broken down en route. Lost title by default in spite of 2–0 first-leg lead.

June 14 Admitted smoking 'pot' to help relax.

June 15 Barred from continental engagements for one month.

June 27 Stopped by police in Leicestershire after motorway chase. Missed his third meeting in a month.

July 12 Booed and jeered during Overseas Final at White City where he struggled to qualify.

August 6 Banned from driving for six weeks.

August 8 Missed home meeting against Hackney because of illness.

August 10 Fined £75 by Leicester magistrates, for possessing cannabis. Threatened with BSPA ban to end of season. Missed more meetings, including Embassy Internationale at Wimbledon and World Team Cup final in West Germany.

August 30 Claimed King's Lynn didn't know how to treat a world champion.

September 6 Asked for transfer from King's Lynn.

October 10 King's Lynn promoter Cyril Crane threatened to sue Lee for loss of revenue and breach of contract.

October 12 Banned for two weeks by BSPA.

October 15 Chipped bone in his back.

Hardly the diary you would hope to see after a year as world champion!

But if **Michael Lee** lost much of his popularity in 1981 he set about regaining his self-respect by courageously agreeing to attend the first British Speedway Supporters Convention, sponsored by *Speedway Star* magazine, at the Norbreck Castle Hotel, Blackpool, in November . . . and to take part in a **Face to Face** interview with *Sunday Express* journalist **Richard Bott**.

He did not dodge any issue as you will see from the transcript of the interview which took place in front of a 'live' audience which included his King's Lynn promoter.

RICHARD BOTT Where did your year as world champion go wrong?

MICHAEL LEE Well, everyone says it's gone wrong but it's not been all bad. I don't know. I think it's been a bad time in general, what with the recession. That seriously affected my earnings and started to get me down. And then my depression reflected on King's Lynn as well.

RICHARD BOTT If you could change some of the things that have happened during the year, what *would* you change?

MICHAEL LEE I've really no regrets. Basically, I enjoyed myself as world champion. Okay, some things have gone wrong and they've been blown up out of all proportion in the Press. People tend to believe the bad rather than the good and that's how you get a bad name.

RICHARD BOTT Would you agree that you have been something of a rebel?

MICHAEL LEE In a way, yes. Nobody in speedway really accepted me as a youngster. I came along as a kid and started beating people and they thought, 'Who's this young upstart?' I won the respect of most of the riders, I think, because I proved I wasn't just a flash in the pan.

I suppose I am a rebel compared with most people. I've always done things my own way and been outspoken and that's got me into trouble at times.

Lee bites the dust at Wembley . . . a sad end to his reign as world champion

RICHARD BOTT That goes back to your schooldays. I've heard a few stories about playing truant. Can you tell us about that?

MICHAEL LEE Out of my last five years of school, I suppose I missed about three. Once I got interested in speedway, that was it. I used to pretend to go to school, then hide behind the bus shelter, run back home, jump in the garage window and start messing about with my bike.

One day the school inspector came round, walked into the garage and there I was, polishing this Jawa. They were going to take me to court and all the teachers thought I was a drop-out. The funny thing is that when I became well known and started to win at speedway, I was invited along to my old school for Speech Day and things like that. So, in the end, you could

say they got me back to school!

But don't get the idea I was dim because I was skipping school. I was quite intelligent. I just couldn't get interested once I was old enough to ride a motor bike.

RICHARD BOTT How did you get started in speedway?

MICHAEL LEE I was thirteen when I got my first speedway bike and I started having rides during the interval at King's Lynn. Not racing, I wasn't old enough. Just riding round. And it all started from there.

RICHARD BOTT Let's come on to your year as world champion. When you were standing on the rostrum in Sweden last year, some of us doubted that you could cope with the pressures of being champion. Do you think, on reflection, that you did win the title too soon?

MICHAEL LEE Maybe so. But I don't think the pressure got to me. It was just a bad year. Financially it didn't come up to expectations. The sponsorship wasn't there the way I had thought it would be for a world champion. That was the basic problem. If the money's not there your interest dims. I suppose that's where it started to go wrong.

RICHARD BOTT In view of what has happened this year, I have to raise the question of drug-taking. We picked up a newspaper one Sunday morning and there was a story saying you took drugs. Now what is your version?

MICHAEL LEE I think everyone believes that the Press blow stories up, particularly if you are in the limelight. It so happens that I was caught with a small amount of cannabis. I'm not ashamed of the fact – there is nothing I can do about it now. But it did result in some bad publicity and I'm sorry that it gave speedway a bad name . . . that is something I hope I can put right in the future.

I have never touched drugs when I have been riding and I'm sure no one else does. It wouldn't be safe. The thing is, what's acceptable in other countries isn't in England. Nobody bats an eyelid about drugs in some places. You travel abroad where habits are different. Then you come home and get into really bad trouble for trying it.

RICHARD BOTT You have had a lot of illness this year. Did this cause you to miss a number of meetings?

MICHAEL LEE Yes, I had a chest complaint and missed three meetings for King's Lynn and they suffered for it. But I was unfit to ride. This was something else that was exaggerated.

I don't think I missed any more meetings during the season than a lot of other top riders – and I didn't miss them on purpose. Speedway is my living. If I don't ride, I don't earn. I don't like letting promoters down . . . or the public. Some of the trouble arose because there were one or two instances when I didn't notify the promoter concerned until late in the day.

RICHARD BOTT But what about the Golden Helmet second leg at Eastbourne. You didn't turn up, you were reported to have broken down and yet the BSPA took the Golden Helmet off you. Why?

MICHAEL LEE Okay, that's probably the worst thing I've done this year. Eastbourne is one of my 'bogy' tracks and I didn't want to ride there. I had won the first leg 2–0 against Gordon Kennett and was prepared to forfeit the second leg and hope to beat him in the decider at Ipswich.

The story that came out at the time was that I'd broken down on the way to Eastbourne but I admit I didn't set off at all.

It was a big mistake on my part and I've apologized to the sponsors, *Motor Cycle News*. I just hope that I get another chance to ride for the Golden Helmet.

RICHARD BOTT On another controversial issue, there has been talk of friction at home and a split from your father, Andy.

MICHAEL LEE There's not really any friction. It was in the Press that we'd had a bust-up but, basically, it's just that my dad was going to move house so I had to find a new workshop. I'm going to be twenty miles away . . . that's all.

RICHARD BOTT What about the King's Lynn situation? Just before the world final I interviewed you at Hull, for the *Sunday Express*, and you claimed the King's Lynn management didn't know how to treat a world champion.

MICHAEL LEE I felt they didn't at the time. But over the whole year I think they have learned a lot about handling a world champion and if it happened again, I'm sure it would be much better.

RICHARD BOTT But in what way do you think they let you down?

MICHAEL LEE I think the world champion should be given weekends off for big meetings. A track should make allowances. I'm sure Hull have for Ivan Mauger, Coventry for Ole Olsen and Cradley for Bruce Penhall. King's Lynn never treated me any differently and I think it was because they'd never had a world champion.

RICHARD BOTT Did things get bitter between you and the King's Lynn management?

MICHAEL LEE Yes, we had a few very heated arguments. Cyril Crane and I have always talked man to man. We've had a good chat this weekend and I think we both regret some of the things quoted in the Press. They didn't do either of us any good. It became a real slanging match at one stage.

RICHARD BOTT Did it affect your riding?

MICHAEL LEE No! When I get on a bike I can shut everything out of my mind.

RICHARD BOTT Do you still want a transfer?

MICHAEL LEE We've talked about it and Cyril has put an offer to me. I've asked him a few questions about what he wants to do with King's Lynn next season. I want to ride for a successful team and this year King's Lynn haven't been one.

RICHARD BOTT But don't you feel you might have let them down?

MICHAEL LEE Yes, certainly. I've missed meetings and had a lot of bad publicity.

RICHARD BOTT How much damage has all the publicity done to your career?

MICHAEL LEE Impossible to judge but, obviously, at the time, a lot of damage. I think people now realize I am not *all* bad. It's not been a good year but it's not been disastrous, results-wise. I finished with a $10\frac{1}{2}$-point average, won the world long-track championship . . .

RICHARD BOTT Was the long-track a chance to stuff the critics or had it always been an ambition of yours?

MICHAEL LEE I went to Radgona with the intention of winning but I didn't really think I stood a chance. The Germans reign supreme on the long track. But after the world speedway final, which was a real disappointment to me, I was determined to make something of the long track.

RICHARD BOTT Do you think you are unpopular?

MICHAEL LEE Yes. If you listen to the crowds around the country I guess I'm pretty unpopular. But I don't mind. The more I get booed, the more determined I am to go out and win.

RICHARD BOTT Are you going to be a different person next season? Are you going to change your attitude towards society, riders, promoters?

MICHAEL LEE I think I've got to. Even during the last two months I think I've quietened down. I don't think you've read too many slanderous words in the Press just recently. If any reporters come on the phone and try to wind me up, I just hang up. I've decided it's better to keep my mouth shut because it's not worth all the trouble it causes. I think I have learned my lesson.

Editor's Note: Early in 1982, Michael Lee withdrew his transfer request and signed a new three-year contract with King's Lynn. He also agreed to take a pay cut to help his team fight the recession!

My clashes with Bruce Penhall
by Kenny Carter
Halifax and England international

You need a lot of luck to become world champion and Bruce Penhall had it so easy last season! But now I'm after his world title. That's my sole ambition. And it's not just because Bruce is the current title holder.

I went to Wembley last September for my first world final appearance, and I went there to win. If I had done, I would have been the youngest-ever champion at twenty. But I didn't have the luck, though I wasn't the only one. Dave Jessup must have felt sicker than me!

An engine failure in my fourth ride finished my hopes when I was looking forward to a heat 20 'decider' with Bruce Penhall. I won that race but he only needed to follow me home to become champion.

I shook hands with him because that's the right thing to do – but I wouldn't say we were the best of friends. Most people think that incident at White City in the overseas final last year was the start of our rivalry. But it goes back further than that.

When I first got started in speedway in 1978, I rode at No 8 for Halifax against Cradley and I trapped on Bruce when he had got a maximum. He tried to pass me on the inside, went on the grass and fell over. He said I chopped him. Ever since then there's been a fair bit of rivalry between us.

I still maintain he put me in the fence at White City last summer, and I'm still furious about it. He came underneath me and shifted me, came again and kept bumping me and took me into the fence. He laid his own bike down to make it look good! He claimed it was an accident but the referee excluded him, quite rightly.

The track interviewer stuck a microphone under my nose and I said exactly what I thought about the incident. That didn't please Bruce or his fans. But how would you feel if someone wrecked your best bike and ripped a pair of boots and a brand new set of leathers worth £200? Would you be pleased?

He not only cost me a lot of money, he could have broken my leg. And he could have put me out of the world championship.

A few words were said on both sides and the Press made a fuss about it before the Inter-continental final in Vojens. I wasn't prepared to take back what I'd said then and I'm not now. But there's no vendetta

. . . you can't afford something like that on a speedway track.

If there was a vendetta, I'd have knocked him off at Halifax when I challenged him for the Golden Helmet!

And don't get me wrong. I don't object to anybody riding hard because that's all part of speedway.

Bruce and I have had a few battles and they get the fans going. But I can't understand the way the Cradley lot carry on when I go there. I guested for Cradley three times last season and scored a maximum, 14 points out of 15 and 11 out of 12. I helped to win them two meetings . . . yet they chuck eggs and abuse at me when I go there to ride against them. They're mental!

I've not done badly in the few years I've been in speedway . . . British Junior champion, British League Riders' champion, Northern Riders' champion, Golden Helmet holder, England international, world finalist etc. But it's not enough.

Somebody asked me if I was surprised I'd done so much so quickly, especially finishing fourth in my first world final. I said I thought it had taken me a long time to achieve that much. I should be world champion by now!

In my first season, at Newcastle in the National League, my bikes were rubbish yet I did all right. If I'd had decent bikes I'd have made better progress. I had a hell of a lot of trouble with overhead cams, otherwise I reckon I'd have reached the 1980 world final in Sweden.

Finishing fourth at Wembley last year did nothing for me. I didn't go there to come fourth, or third or even second. I went there to win – and I was confident because I believed my bikes were as good as anybody's.

Ever since Ivan Mauger first took an interest in me three years ago, I've been asking him to be my manager. And when he got knocked out of the world championship last year, it seemed as good a time as any to try to persuade him. I mean to say, who else could you ask? The bloke has done everything, won everything and been everywhere.

I needed somebody to put me right in a few departments, riding-wise, and to sort things out with promoters and sponsors for me. Apart from anything else, Ivan's got the mechanical know-how and he got my bikes set up properly.

I started off at Wembley on one of my own bikes, knowing I could switch to Ivan's if I wasn't happy. He had loaned me one for the Northern Riders' championship at Sheffield and it was very fast.

Ivan was in the pits with me at Wembley and he was great. I won my first race but my bike started giving me trouble in my next and I had to settle for second place behind Michael Lee. So I switched to Ivan's machine and three points from my next ride meant I still had a good chance and I knew I would be meeting Bruce Penhall in heat 20. So I fancied that to be the 'decider'.

Then it all went wrong in heat 15. When the engine packed up I was heart-broken. I never gave a thought to trying to keep going because I didn't know Dave Jessup was going to pack up as well.

In some ways, I suppose I was lucky to ride at Wembley. Earlier in the season, I smashed my jaw in eight places when I crashed into the fence at Halifax. That was on 4 April when we met Birmingham at The Shay in the League Cup and I clipped Hans Nielsen's wheel. People reckoned I would be out for months but I'd have been

Bruce Penhall appeals against his exclusion at White City

sick if I'd had to pull out of the world championship, so I was back riding again after five weeks!

I rode in the British semi-finals at Sheffield with my jaw wired up. I had no choice. I got 13 points. I had the wire taken out of the jaw two days before the British final at Coventry on 3 June. That night was worse than Sheffield because I was in agony. I couldn't smile and my face was so swollen I could hardly get my helmet on.

I took some pain-killing tablets and got stuck in and nearly won the British championship. My Halifax team-mate John Louis, Swindon's Steve Bastable and I were in a run-off for first place and I finished second. A pity that – but the important thing was qualifying.

Then came the Overseas final at White City and that 'do' with Penhall. He was excluded from the re-run and I got a couple of points to qualify for Vojens . . . but only just. Eight points was pushing it a bit.

Vojens was a better night, even though the conditions were bad. Eleven qualified and I'd done enough after

three rides, though I went on to get 11. Then on to Wembley and you know the rest . . . .

It's funny that I'm talking about wanting to be world champion because I used to think speedway was a rubbish sport! I'd been to a few meetings at Halifax but I wasn't interested in having a go.

You probably know that I come from a motor cycling family. My dad, Malcolm, has always been keen and he sponsors road racer Ron Haslam. Then there's my brother Alan, who is only 17 and he's 'flying' on the road.

But I never really fancied road racing either. I had a go at motocross but I was a bit small for it. Then I went to pre-season practice at Halifax Speedway and won a race. And that's how I got started.

I reckon it's pretty easy. The problem is 'gating'. When I make the 'gate' I don't often get beaten. I had a good winter in Australia and now I'm after that world title!

The Wild West show

Richard Bott *looks ahead to the 1982 World Championship final – the first to be staged in America. The giant Los Angeles Memorial Coliseum, one of the finest stadiums in the world, will house speedway's greatest event just two years before it stages the Olympic Games for the second time. Fans are expected to flock to California from Europe and Australasia. What will be waiting for them?*

The 1982 world final in America is as much a break with tradition as it was twenty-one years ago when the final moved from Wembley for the first time . . . to Malmö, Sweden. It had seemed impossible to envisage a world final anywhere other than at Wembley. From 1936 to 1960, excluding the wartime break, the world's top riders had battled for glory at the famous Empire Stadium.

But after Malmö, Sweden became regular claimants to host the final and then the Poles came on the scene. And in the last decade the championship has moved, in rotation, from Wembley to Katowice to Gothenburg and back to Wembley.

Now the circle has widened and after Los Angeles the championship will move to West Germany, in 1983, before returning to Wembley, its ancestral home.

Los Angeles 1982 promises to be a big adventure . . . for everyone involved, riders,

mechanics, supporters and, not least, the promoters. Three world champions, Jack Milne, Ivan Mauger and Barry Briggs, together with celebrated Californian promoter Harry Oxley, have formed a consortium to stage America's first world championship final.

As Ivan Mauger explains, it is not only the fulfilment of a dream but a massive financial gamble.

'Yes, it's a lot more of a gamble than people think; probably the biggest any of us has taken. Wembley has a ready-made capacity crowd because speedway is big in England. You can always be sure of a big crowd in Poland and Sweden attracts plenty of visitors even though it is such an expensive country.

'Our problem is that speedway does not attract enormous crowds in America and we have to interest people in the States and also try to persuade thousands of fans to travel to Los Angeles from Europe and Australasia.'

The Coliseum seats 105,000 people IN COMFORT. There are no hard wooden benches, every seat has a back to it. But how many of them will be occupied on Saturday 28 August?

Ivan Mauger says: 'We may need around 45,000 to break even . . . it depends on television fees and sponsorships. We appreciate that thousands of people will not be able to travel to America so we are trying to make sure that more people see this world final on TV than ever before.

'Terms have already been agreed with ITV in England and CBS in America. Now we are looking to other countries to buy TV rights. It means knocking on a few doors in Europe and Australasia and that will be one of my jobs in the coming months.

'Why did we pick the Coliseum? Simple. It has the same kind of status as Wembley. We looked at several other venues in California, including Los Angeles. But the Coliseum is the right shape and it is world-famous . . . like Wembley.

'The world final is in West Germany in 1983 and my only criticism of the Germans is that they are staging the final at Norden. It is one of my favourite tracks and they are putting up new stands. But in my opinion Norden does not have the status. IT WILL DEVALUE THE WORLD CHAMPIONSHIP!

'Why can't the Germans put the final on at the Olympic Stadium in Munich? They could do what we have done in Los Angeles . . . lay a speedway track over the tartan running track. The 1984 Olympic Games will be held in the Los Angeles Coliseum but that hasn't stopped the authorities allowing us to put down a speedway track. And we have done nothing that the Germans couldn't do.

'When you build a speedway track from new, provided the shape is right, you can make sure it is perfect. The people we employed to build the track in Los Angeles knew nothing about speedway but they did the job in fourteen days! Nobody knows better than Barry Briggs and myself what is required and we advised the workmen accordingly.

Jack Milne, America's first world champion in 1937, points to his picture in a cigarette card collection of former speedway superstars

'We have already staged a major meeting on the track, which we had to do to satisfy the FIM. The 1981 American final was raced there and Charles Ringblom gave the track a glowing report.

'LA in 1982 is the fulfilment of a dream. Some people have complained about the final going to America, just as others complained about it going to Sweden and then to Poland. Well, I've ridden in fourteen speedway finals and I've never complained about the venue as such . . . because when you have a world championship the operative word is *WORLD*!

'Why should one or two countries have a monopoly. Let's have the final in Italy or France or Yugoslavia . . . provided the stadium has the status required.'

There is no question that the Coliseum fits the bill. In California they call it 'the hub of the biggest wheel in the world' because it stands in the centre of the city with the largest land area in the world.

55

The Coliseum was built around an abandoned gravel pit and as a memorial to the brave men who lost their lives in the First World War. Work began in 1921 and the stadium was completed in June 1923 – incidentally the year Wembley Stadium staged the first FA Cup final!

And like Wembley, the Los Angeles Memorial Coliseum has staged everything you can think of . . . and plenty you can't . . . conventions, pop concerts, horse shows, political rallies, professional boxing, rodeos, ski jumping, midget car racing, American grid-iron football, religious services, Christmas pageants, the Olympic Games – in 1932 – and, would you believe, speedway!

Yes, sometime in the days of deep dirt tracks and leg-trailing, I cannot discover the actual year, speedway made its bow in the great man-made bowl.

The next occasion was the American Final of the 1981 World Championship, on Saturday 30 May. And, appropriately, it was America's next world champion, Bruce Penhall, who christened the new 400-metre track with a 15-points maximum.

They always say that everything is bigger and better in the States. Well, here are a few statistics about the Coliseum to compare with other arenas:

30 miles and 79 rows of seating

Overall area of Coliseum grounds: 27 acres

74 turnstiles

90 entrances

Cost of original construction: 800,000 dollars plus a further 1,800,000 dollars in 1931

Dressing room facilities for 275 people

Last row of seats 106 feet above ground level

Press box 230 feet long and seating 225 media representatives

One statistic I cannot reveal is the cost of hiring this magnificent arena for the 1982 world final but Ivan Mauger says: 'If you think Wembley is expensive to rent, try hiring the Coliseum! Wembley costs only a fraction of what our consortium has paid for the Coliseum. But we are determined to prove we have done the right thing.

'We have been working towards this world final since 1976. Barry Briggs and myself have always had individual ideas on how a world final should be run and we will be putting those ideas into practice along with Harry Oxley and Jack Milne.

'We know the gripes a rider can have when it comes to a world final, regarding organization of travel, practice timetables, position in the pits etc. We won't be holding

The famous Los Angeles Memorial Coliseum which will stage the 1982 World final

people by the hand but we will try to use our years of experience.'

Ivan promises a world final to remember and reveals: 'We have decided to have a Wild West theme! After all, California is the west and that means cowboys and indians, stage coaches and the rest. And the final must have a genuine American flavour in terms of showmanship and entertainment.

'But as far as the racing itself goes, we will do it strictly by the book.'

But will the fans flock to California or not? Ivan says: 'British speedway fans think nothing of going to Poland or Sweden, and there is no need for America to scare them off.

'Look at the number of fans who fly to Warsaw and then trek down to Katowice or go the whole way by boat and train.

The Los Angeles Coliseum is eight miles from the airport so the only travelling problem is that you have to spend a bit longer on an aeroplane.

'Once you get to America the food and accommodation is so much cheaper than Europe and hotels usually have two double beds in a room and children stay free of charge. You don't have to stay for a fortnight. It's possible to fly to Los Angeles, arrive a couple of hours before the meeting, stay one night and fly back the next morning. People should forget about the distance involved, it's no real sweat.'

If you do go, you're in for the experience of a lifetime . . . that lovely Californian sunshine...Hollywood...Disneyland... Pacific prawns and juicy steaks . . . and speedway's first-ever WILD WEST SHOW!

Denmark rules OK

Hans Nielsen, *who rides in the British League for Birmingham, is the reigning World Masters Champion and helped Denmark to win the World Team Cup in Olching, West Germany, in August 1981. Here he suggests Denmark will rule world speedway for a number of years.*

I think that we have the best team Denmark has ever had and that we will win the World Team Cup for many years to come. That is a good possibility, anyway. England will be the biggest threat but our team is very young and more good riders are coming up.

The introduction of 50cc speedway racing in Denmark is the reason for our great progress in the last few years. This all started after Ole Olsen won his first world championship, in 1971. There is no question that Ole has done a lot for Danish speedway and is still a very good rider and team captain.

I started riding on 50cc motor bikes in my home town of Brovst, in Northern Denmark, when I was thirteen years old, eight years ago. My two older brothers were speedway riders. One of them, Henry, spent a month with Swindon Robins last season. He could have come to England before but he is not really all that interested in speedway.

In Denmark you do not get money for riding in speedway, except in the big international meetings at Vojens. The racing is for amateurs although we have quite a lot of teams now, sixteen in the First Division and sixteen in the Second.

You can ride 50cc bikes when you are twelve and 500cc at the age of sixteen. The little bikes are used on small tracks, about 200 yards round, but it is the same as real speedway . . . you learn how to slide the bike and to race. It is because of this kind of riding that so many good young riders are coming through and making Danish speedway stronger.

I won the Danish Junior Championship in 1976, my first year on 500cc bikes. Then Wolverhampton said they wanted me to ride for them and I came to England. The only thing that worried me was leaving school about three months before I should have done!

I wanted to have a go at speedway in England, so I came over to Wolverhampton very determined to do well. I had a fairly good first season in the British League, in 1977, with an average of over seven points per meeting. The second season my average was up to 8.85 and that was a very good season because I became Danish Senior Champion and also was a

Delighted Danes give Erik Gundersen the traditional bumps after he has assured them of World Cup victory

member of the team that won the World Team Cup for the first time.

We reached the final by finishing runners-up to England at Belle Vue. Sweden did not qualify. Our team for the final in Landshut, West Germany, was Ole Olsen, Finn Thomsen, Mike Lohmann and myself with Kristian Praestbro at reserve. I was the top scorer in the final, with 11 points. That was a very special day for Danish speedway . . . and for me!

I think my performance there came as a bit of a surprise to everybody, including me, and it gave me a bit of confidence. But we lost the 1979 World Cup final at White City, finishing second to New Zealand. I scored nine points in that meeting.

The big moment for me in 1979 was helping Ole Olsen to win the World Pairs final at Vojens. Ole scored 15 points and I got 10 and we beat England – Michael Lee and Malcolm Simmons – by one point. That was the first time Denmark had ever won the Pairs championship.

My time at Wolverhampton was not very happy because the team was not successful. I rode for them until the end of the 1980 season but then I moved to Birmingham. We did not win anything last year but Dan McCormick, the promoter,

59

does a lot for the riders and to finish sixth in the British League was much better than Wolverhampton had done.

I have not done very well in the World Individual Championship, so far. My first final was in Gothenburg, in 1980, and I scored seven points. That was not too bad because everything was new to me. A world final is very different from any other meeting. Gothenburg was bad only because of the track. You had to make good starts every time to have a chance.

Wembley, last year, was very disappointing but I had some bad luck. I was fairly happy after finishing second in my first race and I gated quite well in my second, when I was out with Bruce Penhall, Ole Olsen and Egon Muller. Penhall sort of pushed me a bit and I drifted wide and couldn't get back in the race. When you finish last in a race in the world final, you know you can't win the meeting so you really don't have anything to fight for after that.

Also, my bike had lost some compression and I wasn't fast enough.

I cannot explain why I have not done very much in the world championship so far. The other Danish riders were magnificent at Wembley and I am sure that we will have a Danish world champion again in the next year or two. I believe I can do well because I have won the World Masters Championship twice and some other individual meetings, like the Embassy Internationale. Maybe I have not made the starts so far in World Finals.

The worst time in the World Team Cup was at Vojens in 1980, when England and America knocked us out in front of our own crowd. Everything seemed to go wrong for us that night. It is very difficult when you have three very strong teams, like England and America and Denmark. It is good they are changing the rule in 1983 so that the third team in the Inter-continental final can still qualify for the world final.

Why did we win in 1981 in Olching? I think we had the best team and also the team spirit was very good, which is important. We had different riders from when we won in 1978 but we all got on really well before the meeting and at the practice.

We had a good team manager, Olaf Pedersen, and Ole has the experience and is a big help to the other riders. It would be worth having him in the team even if he was not scoring a lot of points!

Before the final we were staying in a nice hotel beside a river and went swimming. We just relaxed and had a good time and that helped to make us confident. I am sure that another advantage we had over England was that their team manager was not with them for the practice. There has been a lot of talk about that but I feel it is important for the manager to be there.

Now Denmark can go on winning. We have a young team apart from Ole. Erik Gundersen and I are twenty-two, Tommy Knudsen is twenty, Bo Petersen is twenty-four, and Finn Thomsen twenty-seven. In the past, we did not have many riders to choose from but now we have a young team that can go on for some time yet . . . and I expect some more talent to come through.

Junior riders in England do not get much opportunity to practise but they do in Denmark. Danish speedway has never been so well off for good riders as it is now.

Above **World champions again! The triumphant Danes on the rostrum at Olching**
Below **Close encounter in the qualifying round at King's Lynn. Dennis Sigalos (USA) and Hans Nielsen fight for the lead**

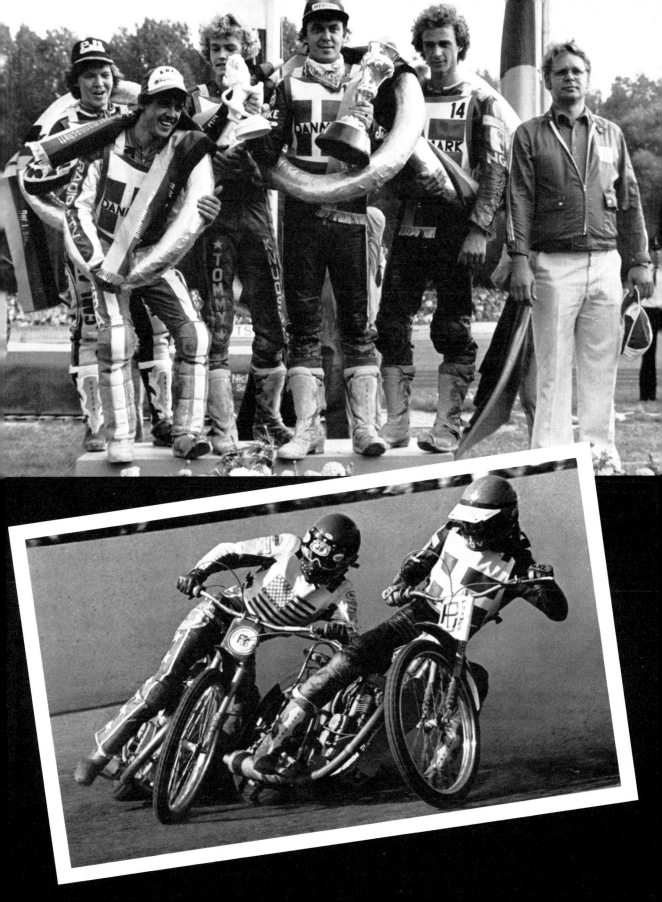

Safety first...but is it?

Richard Bott *was in Vojens, Denmark, to cover the 1981 Inter-continental Final of the World Championship for the Sunday Express. Torrential rain caused the meeting to be abandoned after four heats, only to be resumed amid a storm of controversy ninety-five minutes later. Fourteen of the sixteen riders voted to have the meeting postponed for twenty-four hours. They were overruled. Should officials have the authority to gamble with the lives of the riders to appease the promoters and the fans? Do they really put safety first?*

England's former world champion Peter Collins was not in Vojens last July but a few months later, during a discussion on Rider Safety, he made some frightening observations.

'If you really want to know what it is like riding a speedway bike on a very wet track,' he said, 'get into your car tonight, find a nice fast stretch of motorway and close your eyes for a few seconds!

'Then try to imagine turning a corner at the same speed, still with your eyes closed. And, remember, that in that kind of situation, a speedway rider cannot take his hands off the handle-bars to remove his goggles!'

P.C. was, in no way, seriously advocating that his audience should risk life and limb and that of other road users. And it is accepted that anyone who rides speedway *does* take risks. But how great should those risks be? And should a referee be forced to take a greater risk than the riders? After all, if he passes a track fit and a rider is killed, who takes the blame?

Many speedway meetings *are* called off and there are as many arguments over these as the ones that are allowed to start or to continue.

But it is an indisputable fact that the more important the meeting, e.g. a world championship final, the more reluctant are the authorities to call it off and the more pressure there is on the referee who, under the regulations, has to make the final decision.

I have seen the Ullevi Stadium track in Gothenburg turned into a lake during a world final. Yet the meeting has been completed. I have been at Coventry on British final night when the rain has poured down and officials and riders have deliberated at length when the only correct decision was to call the meeting off.

But the Inter-continental final of the

Fourteen of the 16 riders at Vojens wanted the meeting called off. Denmark's Ole Olsen, pictured here with Cliff Andersson, voted to continue

1981 World Championship was a classic case. Vojens, the stadium that was the brainchild of Denmark's first world champion, Ole Olsen, is a magnificent and thoroughly worthy venue for any top international event.

And it is desperately sad that in the past three seasons, practice-day sunshine has given way to leaden skies and a downpour. Having to postpone or abandon a big international meeting creates administrative havoc. Riders and officials have other commitments, spectators may have travelled hundreds of miles on charter flights due to return soon after the meeting.

But after what happened at Vojens last July, I have the feeling that rider safety is no longer the primary concern of the organizers. The priority now would appear to be RUN AT ALL COSTS!

Remember that the Inter-continental final was the last stepping-stone to Wembley for the 16 riders. All their efforts and ambitions had been channelled into qualifying for the world final and this 'semi-final' would have been testing enough on a dry track.

Well, it *was* dry at the start. Although rain had been forecast all day and was, reportedly, only a few miles away, the promoters insisted on having an unnecessarily long parade. As a result, the rain started to fall heavily during a fourth heat that was bizarre enough without the intervention of the weather.

In that race, the Polish referee, Roman Cheladze, who had made a couple of strange decisions earlier, failed to notice that the starting gate had dropped during the first lap. He allowed the riders to spear through the tapes at the start of the second lap and still refused to stop the race!

But that incident paled into insignifi-

cance alongside what happened later.

The rain came down in buckets after Bruce Penhall had won that fourth heat. And it kept falling. A reasonable delay was understandable. But as the conditions continued to deteriorate and a remarkably patient 21,000 crowd, most of them out in the open, waited for the rain to abate, the time dragged on and the arguments became more and more heated.

After an hour it seemed logical that the meeting must be called off. A re-run the following day was the solution. Or at least it should have been.

But by now there was utter confusion and the verbal bullets started to fly.

As riders, mechanics and officials

Eric Boocock, appointed England team manager this season, and a former world finalist with considerable experience of wet conditions, was furious that no interpreter was available in the pits to converse with the non-English-speaking referee.

Referee Cheladze spoke Polish and German and the riders were not happy that the only interpreter available was a Danish official who clearly had the interests of the organizers at heart. And, equally clearly, the organizers and officials were determined to go ahead with the meeting because, when the rain eased, they piled tons of sand and limestone dust on the track to soak up the water.

Then they sent out four Danish riders, stand-by reserves, for a test run. But that was a farce in itself. The riders did not *race*, they merely made starts and followed each other round the sodden circuit.

But the most damning indictment of the decision to resume, ninety-five minutes after the initial stoppage, was the vote taken at a riders' meeting. Fourteen said 'No' to a request to re-start, two said 'Yes', Ole Olsen and Preben Eriksen.

Olsen, trying desperately to remain impartial when he could not be, as co-promoter of the meeting as well as one of the participants, found himself berated from all sides. One rider told me: 'He can speak German and he's been telling the referee to get the meeting on again. We want it off.'

Well, the riders didn't have their way. Nor did they make a sufficient stand – even though they were gambling their world championship hopes and, more to the point, their lives!

huddled under cover in the pits, BSPA president and FIM delegate Jack Fearnley told me: 'It is scandalous that riders of this quality should be expected to race in these conditions. Apart from the safety factor, months of sweat and toil can be ruined. Ninety thousand people are going to Wembley to see the lads who qualify from here . . . and the meeting has been turned into a lottery.

'The trouble is the people out here are not speedway-orientated like us. They are just beginners. It was an error to start at 8.20 p.m. An afternoon meeting would have given the promoters a bit of leeway in the case of bad weather. Now they find themselves in trouble.'

Olsen was angry and frustrated by the accusations and the delay. He felt the referee should have made a decision earlier. He felt also that riders who would have accepted such conditions in England were now looking for excuses.

As you are well aware, the meeting did resume and, thankfully, no one was seriously hurt. In fact, in fairness, the conditions improved towards the end of the meeting and the race times were reasonable.

But is that sufficient justification for the referee overruling a 14–2 vote?

Bruce Penhall, who won the event with a 15-points maximum, said afterwards: 'It was the referee's decision to go ahead but I feel the riders should have a lot more say in the future. It should be up to us whether we race or not. It's okay for the ref sitting up in his dry box. We are the guys who have to risk our necks!

'I felt sorry for the public but the track *was* dangerous. When the riders met the referee I had three points from my first ride. But I went along with the majority that the track wasn't fit after the rain.

'I made five great starts but it must have been terrible for the guys at the back. They had no chance of passing in conditions like that.

'The referee didn't speak any English and his interpreter was a top Danish official. That's all wrong, in my opinion. If the referee can't speak to the riders directly, how can he overrule them?

'It upset me that the officials blamed Ivan Mauger for trying to get the meeting called off. He was our elected representative, because of his experience. He did not try to influence us. Most of us decided the track was unsafe.'

George Barclay, former rider and secretary of the SRA, makes no bones about the basic issue. He says: 'when you ride on a wet track and you are not at the front, you can't see. You are riding "blind". AND THAT IS DANGEROUS!"

The next time you go to a speedway meeting and it rains, remember those words . . . particularly if you are the referee!

Riders and officials argue with Polish referee Roman Cheladze at Vojens

The fifty points farce

Ian Thomas, *co-promoter of Hull Lada Vikings and Newcastle Lada Diamonds in 1981 and team manager of England when they achieved a unique Grand Slam in 1980, is totally opposed to speedway's 50-points rule which has operated in the British League for three seasons and has been introduced to the National League regulations for 1982.*

The object of the rule is to ensure that teams are not able to become over-powerful and to create a situation in which riders are made available to teams in need. **Ian Thomas** *not only believes such a restriction is wrong but has proved the rule can be manipulated . . . as he explains here.*

Take three world champions . . . Ivan Mauger, Peter Collins and Michael Lee . . . plus three more top-line international speedway stars . . . Kenny Carter, Phil Crump and Dave Jessup. Add any current National League rider with an average of five points.

Put those seven riders together and you have a team that could LEGALLY compete in the National League, despite the new 50-points rule!

Crazy? Yes. Impossible? Not on paper. I will prove to you that six world-class British League riders plus one average, middle-of-the-road National League man could legitimately operate as a team in the National League.

Yet that same collection of riders could NOT operate as a team in the British League, where a 50-point limit has been in force for three seasons! Now isn't that farcical?

Because of a loophole in the law, as it affects National League tracks, six riders with a total British League average of 59.32 (based on the 1981 green sheets) only add up to 45 points when it comes to National League!

If you – and some of my fellow promoters – are scratching your heads and thinking Thomas has a screw loose, let me present you with the facts and the possibilities.

The first point to take into consideration is this. It is a National League rule that if a rider has been out of that league for more than two seasons, i.e. riding for a team in the British League, and wants to return to the National League, he is given an assessed average of 7.50.

Therefore, the top riders I listed, Mauger, Collins, Lee, Carter, Crump and Jessup, would be assessed at 7.50 – IF they moved down.

If you know your rulebook you will argue that this could never happen because any rider who wants a move from British League to National League has first to be circulated to all BL promoters. Agreed. And these riders would be snapped up.

Now we find the loophole in the law. If you know you have a rider at British League level who you know will be snapped up as soon as you circulate his name, you fix him up with another British League club as their No. 8 and have him 'loaned' to your National League track! That is a perfectly legal way around one of the problems of BEATING THE 50-POINTS RULE IN NATIONAL LEAGUE.

Okay. I know that, realistically, no British League or National League promoter could afford to pay the wages of the riders I have named, let alone to buy them. In exposing one of the loopholes I have taken it to ridiculous lengths.

But you will now begin to understand how I was able to beat the 50-point rule at Newcastle this year AND sign two British League riders, Joe Owen and Bobby Beaton!

The 50-points rule is supposed to help teams in need. But, in my opinion, it does not work. Usually, a team in need is not a wealthy one so the transfer fees required by a team with a 50-points problem prevent the weaker teams from buying the better quality riders.

While the 50-point rule was supported by a very large majority of National League promoters at the annual conference, I personally voted against it for the following reasons: 1) in 1981 the British League was virtually a two-horse race all season, even with a 50-points rule; 2) in the same season the National League was a four or five horse race until the end of the season, without a 50-points rule! 3) the financial position of certain clubs will prevent the rule from

working at National League level and, as a result, put several riders in the dole queue; 4) my own team, Newcastle Lada Diamonds, was left with a 50-points problem!

For the past seven years I have promoted tracks in both the National League and the British League. And I don't accept the criticism of several British League promoters that National League tracks hang on to their best riders.

The reason why so many good National League riders do not move up into the senior league is because they feel they are better off where they are. And that is partially due to the British League promoters, or some of them, persisting in recruiting low-grade foreign riders. Another reason is that the top two or three riders in a British League team take the bulk of the money available and since that does not leave much for the second strings, the National League boys feel they are better off where they are.

But the really ambitious ones are prepared to take a gamble and move up, anyway. David Bargh, a young New Zealander with a nine-points average at Newcastle last year, made it clear at the end of the season that he wanted to try his luck in the British League. So he would have left us whatever the circumstances.

Newcastle Lada Diamonds finished the 1981 National League season with a combined average of 61.04, the highest in the competition. But that figure included my captain, Tom Owen, at 11.04 – his 1979 average because he rode only two matches in 1980 and one in 1981.

After the annual conference decision to bring in the 50-points rule, I succeeded in persuading the National League management committee and then the General

Above **Newcastle Lada Diamonds promoter Ian Thomas, seen here with former world champions Ivan Mauger and Barry Briggs at the Lada Indoor International, slams the 50-point rule**
Right **Sheffield promoter Ray Glover believes Shawn Moran, his American thunderbolt, is his best-ever signing**

Council to give Tom Owen an assessed average of 7.50 for 1982, if he was fit to return to league racing.

Of course this helped me to beat the 50-point rule and it made history because Tom Owen is the first rider to have his average reduced in such a way. But I also believed it was morally unfair for a man who had missed two seasons and had four operations on his leg, to be burdened with such an average.

Anyway, with Tom's average reduced to 7.50, I was able to sign Joe Owen and Bobby Beaton from Hull, by attaching each of them to a British League track and having them 'loaned' out to Newcastle!

When Joe Owen left Newcastle for Hull at the end of the 1976 season, he was the top rider in the National League, with an average of 11.55. And he is now a better rider, or should be after five years in the British League. Yet the rulebook allows me to take him back to Newcastle at an assessed average of 7.50!

Bobby Beaton, who has never ridden in the National League, averaged 5.45 for Hull last year. But I would class him as a nine or ten points a meeting man in the National League.

The other new rule which has helped me is the one which says no National League rider can have an average of less than two points. In other words, his average is assessed at two even if it is less than that in reality or if he has not yet attained a genuine average. The important fact, from my point of view, is that in British League the lowest assessed average is 3.00. And that one point made all the difference when I prepared my 1982 Newcastle line-up and concerned a young rider called Paul McHale.

So I pencilled in the following team for 1982 with their legitimate averages, assessed or otherwise:

Tom Owen (7.50), Joe Owen (7.50), Bobby Beaton (7.50), Robbie Blackadder (8.64), Alan Emerson (8.57), Keith Bloxsome (7.61), Paul McHale (2.00). Total average: 49.32

But let us suppose that Tom Owen had stayed at 11.04 and Joe Owen at his old National League average of 11.55, Bobby Beaton at his potential NL average of 10 points and Paul McHale at three points . . . then the total would have been 60.41! And that's only half a point worse off than 1981!

So, without breaking any rules or regulations, I have found a way round the 50-point rule and, hopefully, ensured that the Newcastle public will again see a team with the potential to win the championship.

Hull Lada Vikings suffered from a 50-point problem for two years in the British League. I attacked that by forming a pool of riders and leaving the top ones out in rotation. In 1981 Hull had no such problem but again I opposed the rule. So no one can accuse me of wearing two hats.

But I tried to when the National League rule was brought in. I made a serious attempt to close all the loopholes in case somebody like me exposed them. And, bluntly, I don't believe they can be closed. Not all of them. But I'm keeping a few up my sleeve!

And I'm quite convinced that, in taking Joe Owen and Bobby Beaton to Newcastle for 1982, I haven't exploited loophole No. 1 to its full potential. That should be obvious from my opening comments.

The title of this chapter is *The Fifty Points Farce*. Well, to make the rule work every track has to believe in it – and they don't!

SOME OF THE PROMOTERS WHO VOTED TO INTRODUCE THE RULE IN 1982 HAVE ASKED ME WAYS TO BEAT IT. AND IF THAT DOESN'T MAKE THE WHOLE THING A FARCE, I DON'T KNOW WHAT DOES!

Another thing . . . although I was one of three promoters to oppose the introduction of the 50-points rule, the other members of the National League management committee asked *me* to draw up the appendix to the regulations!

But I have no conscience about finding a loophole in the law and exploiting it. The powers that be tried to knock the stuffing out of my Newcastle team. Maybe they helped me to come up with a better one!

Speedway world wide

Yes, Speedway is truly international and has been from the pioneering days when top English stars like Frank Varey and Eric Langton sailed to South America to become as popular on the other side of the Atlantic as they were here.

The British League remains the biggest, the best and the most cosmopolitan. Our promoters help to create world champions for other nations by bringing their riders over here and giving them the opportunity to reach top class.

Ipswich promoter and England co-ordinator John Berry says: 'Whilst we are training everybody else's riders we are helping England to get beaten. But is that such a disaster when it creates healthy world competition?'

English fans can hardly complain because they see the highest level of competition week after week.

But speedway is spreading its wings. Nine-times world champion Ivan Mauger has raced in twenty-six countries and that gives you some idea of the growth of speedway over the years. North and South America, Europe, Australasia, Africa, the Middle East, even Japan, where they race on banked tarmac tracks. Where will the sport cross its next frontier?

American Bobby Schwartz watches a steamroller iron out the bumps at Rijswijk in Holland

How many British tracks have palm trees?
This is speedway California-style, at San
Bernardino
Left Young Poland in action at Oxford on
their British tour in 1981. The Oxford
rider is Dave Perks

Don't shoot the ref... he's only human!
by Richard Bott

Anyone who becomes a referee, whether it be football, boxing, tennis, speedway, must have masochistic tendencies! No one can enjoy being abused and vilified by competitors, team managers and spectators, unless he has a warped sense of humour or a skin as tough as buffalo hide.

Mind you, on the credit side there is the self-satisfaction of being in control, having the last word, calling the tune. Power and independence.

In two paragraphs I have given you the two extremes. When it comes down to brass tacks a good referee need no more be abused than feel superior. What he must be, at all times, is responsible.

Speedway referees in Great Britain are appointed by the Speedway Control Board which is a body representing the interests of the Auto-Cycle Union in this particular sport. Briefly, the referee's job is 'to ensure that a meeting is conducted in accordance with the Speedway Regulations'.

But it takes up nearly 1000 words and nine clauses to define the duties of a referee in the Speedway Control Board handbook. For very little financial reward, the referee has to make vital decisions about track conditions before and during a meeting, starting procedure, incidents occurring during races, protests by riders and team managers etc etc. And he often has to make these decisions under some very trying conditions and, invariably, under extreme pressure.

And, at the end of the day, he can't win! If he has done a good job and there have been no serious problems, nothing to antagonize the riders or the public, who cares? Isn't that what he is there for? But if he has been the centre of a storm and has had to make a decision or several decisions that have upset one side or the other, he is the big bad wolf!

I wonder if the majority of speedway fans, for all their knowledge of the sport, really appreciate the problems facing a speedway referee. For one thing, he remains something of a 'ghost' figure, away from the action, out of sight. In the majority of sports, the referee is *visible* to the crowd. At a speedway meeting, he often sits in a commentary box on the roof of the stand or similarly enclosed at the back of the stand where he is visible only to a few supporters.

His vantage point can be good, bad or indifferent. A stanchion may obscure his view of the first or last bend. He may be at an angle to the starting gate, making it very

It's the Starting Marshal's job to help the referee by making sure all four riders are in line and stationary. In this picture Paul Johnson checks on the riders at the start of heat 20 in the 1981 World final

difficult to judge a photo finish or to guarantee a fair start. The track lighting may be inadequate. The telephone, his link with pits, centre green or announcer's box, may not be functioning properly.

For an insight into the problems of the men who we tend to take for granted or abuse mercilessly, let us listen to some of the views of three top Auto-Cycle Union referees, **John Whitaker**, **Lew Stripp** and **Jack Miller**.

JOHN WHITAKER If the starts are good the meeting usually goes like clockwork. Incidents on the track don't happen all that often but every single speedway meeting

the referee has to make twenty or so starts. It is how he handles them that makes or mars a meeting.

It is a referee's responsibility to make sure that all four riders get a fair start. But it is the individual rider's responsibility to try to get a better start than the other three in the race. And this leads to conflicts.

In my opinion, the only way to give them all a fair chance is to hold the tapes for long enough to let them all settle down. This can be frustrating for a rider but at least he knows that it is just as frustrating for his opponents. If the referee lets the tapes go up too quickly it can lead to riders later attempting to cheat, then everyone feels they've got to try to cheat and the whole meeting degenerates into a shambles.

You have to give riders time to settle at the tapes because there is a lot of tension. Nerves can affect the best riders. And I know for a fact that it is an unbelievable sensation to sit on a speedway bike at the start, with something like 70–80 horse power underneath you, and go from 0–70 mph on the space of a few seconds.

Supporters get very annoyed about various antics at the start but some of them cannot be helped. A rider's goggles tend to steam up on a cold night. Often, when this happens, you will see a rider pull out of his start position and wipe his goggles. That is not necessarily gamesmanship. And I certainly won't allow four riders to go into the first bend at 70mph if I think they can't see!

Another important factor concerns tape-breaking. I contend that the tape will break at its *weakest* point, not necessarily where it has been pushed forward! And this can lead to supporters thinking the referee has excluded the wrong rider.

If more than one rider is pushing the

tapes when they break I like to see all four go back in. But when tapes do break, everyone has a different point of view.

Should a referee ever change his decision? Yes, if he thinks he has made the wrong one then he must correct it. Very rarely I have done this, sometimes as a result of some information given over the pits phone.

The most common mistake a referee can make is to switch on the wrong exclusion light or to put on the red exclusion light instead of the red stop light. It's very easy to move a switch unintentionally when you are watching the race, particularly when the switch panels vary so much from track to track.

At one track in the north, the panel of light switches is virtually over the referee's shoulder. At other tracks it is in front of you, like the console of an organ. Because of these different conditions, it is not uncommon to make a mistake but it makes me very cross because I regard it as a stupid mistake on my part.

When it comes to an incident during a race, I think it pays to pause for a few seconds, to re-run it through your mind and then make your decision. Bear in mind that a referee can only make a decision on what *he* sees, not what the rider sees, or the team manager or the bloke on the terraces.

If he sees it wrongly, then he will make the wrong decision. But he has to have the final say. And for all the talk of having someone else down on the start or on the bends, I'm a firm believer in having one man in charge.

LEW STRIPP I don't change my mind very often – a couple of times in twelve years – and afterwards, I've thought back on it and decided my first instinct was the right one.

Some supporters get the impression the referee has changed his mind because he accidentally puts the wrong exclusion light on. What they tend to forget is that we often have to work in the pitch dark during a race, so it's very easy to press the wrong switch.

What causes a lot of aggravation with the public is lack of information. They don't mind delays if they are kept informed.

When it comes to starts, I always rule an unsatisfactory start if the tapes break on the way up. I believe that once I have released the starting gate, the riders are entitled to go!

You get a fair amount of physical contact on the first corner and I feel the riders accept that. We don't want to see the riders queuing up to go into the first turn like they do in road racing. That's the big difference. There's always going to be a bit of pushing and shoving.

The forms that are used to give referees marks for how they have handled the meeting are a joke. I've had them handed to me before a meeting with the marks filled in already!

JACK MILLER It's easy enough for a referee to give all four riders the benefit of the doubt if something happens on the first lap. But if it happens on the last lap he has to take a decision and be very positive.

Riders – and referees – accept a bit of pushing and jostling on the first turn as par for the course in a physical sport. Here Cradley's Phil Collins fights to tuck in behind team-mate Alan Grahame

One great problem is that on every track, there is one very bad corner from a referee's point of view. The third turn is the worst corner for a referee to have a proper view of what is happening.

I accept that if a referee presses the wrong exclusion button, he has made a mistake and must correct it. But, in my four years as a referee, I have never changed my decision about an incident in a race. If you do, you are immediately put under pressure by riders, team managers etc, and the situation becomes chaotic.

Once I have made up my mind who is to blame, that incident is over as far as I'm concerned. Nobody will change my mind. And I make the decision on the strength of what I have seen.

One problem is created for us by the use of the word 'immediately' in the rulebook. In Regulation 210, which refers to 'Foul or Dangerous Riding', it says 'The referee shall exclude IMMEDIATELY a rider who, in his opinion, indulges in foul, unfair or dangerous conduct . . . .'

That word is a bit unfortunate. I think there is a lot of merit in a referee pausing for a few seconds before making a decision. I know of last-lap incidents when the riders have been over the finishing line before the referee has made his decision. Then the team manager is justified in saying that the referee did not exclude IMMEDIATELY the rider who caused the problem.

So there you have it . . . a few opinions about some of the problems and duties of the men in charge.

Often the referee has to make his most important decision before the riders ever come to the tapes . . . whether a track is fit for racing or not. He has the power to postpone or abandon a meeting but only after consultation with the Clerk of the Course, the respective team managers and team captains.

This particular problem is discussed at greater length elsewhere in the *Lada International Speedway Book* since it was highlighted by the controversy which surrounded the Inter-continental final of the world championship in Denmark last summer. The language barrier can be a particular problem and caused a good deal of the trouble on that occasion.

Communication is vital and a good referee will always have a word with the riders before the start of a meeting to familiarize them with his methods.

Finally, let us examine the disciplinary powers of a referee.

Did you know that the maximum fine he can impose is £50? But in the event of a serious breach of the regulations, further action can be taken by the Speedway Control Board.

Fines of up to £50 can be imposed by the referee for the following:
Disorderly or ungentlemanly conduct
Failure to acknowledge authority
Unauthorized commentary
Failing to comply with instructions given by the referee
Dissent
Absence from a meeting
Team without a team manager

Fines of up to £25 for:
Failure to withdraw from the course
Team under strength

Fines of up to £20 for:
Late arrival
Malingering (not trying to win)
Approved-type helmet not bearing ACU stamp
Any unauthorized person delaying start of a race
Withdrawing or attempting to withdraw a rider or team
Refusal to ride

Fines of up to £10 for:
Unauthorized approach to the referee
Rider delaying the start of a race
Proceeding to the start of a race in the opposite direction to the course
Not complying with the instructions of the Starting Marshal
Failing to wear identification disc
Intoxicants
Failing to wear a correct body colour
Motor cycle not complying with the regulations

More serious offences which are likely to be dealt with by a Speedway Control Board disciplinary tribunal include:
Improper comment
Conduct prejudicial to the sport
Employment of a rider not under agreement
Leaving a meeting without permission
Illegal payments

But the next time you go to watch your favourite team try to remember that referees don't make the rules, they only enforce them. They may be there to be shot down . . . but they're only human!

Indoor pioneers

Where do Speedway fans go in the winter? Lada Cars came up with an answer in December 1979 when they pioneered Indoor Speedway in Britain. And the gamble they took in sponsoring an international meeting at Wembley Arena, paid off handsomely. **Richard Bott** *traces the development of indoor racing at home and abroad and looks at the possibilities for the future.*

Wembley is a magical name to anyone with a knowledge of or a taste for speedway racing. It conjures up a picture of world finals, great nights and high drama. So Ivan Mauger, Barry Briggs and Ian Thomas had 'a starter for ten' when they made their initial plans to launch indoor racing at the famous Wembley Arena.

Jan Andersson's crouching style takes him clear of England's Steve Bastable in the 1981 Lada Indoor International Match Race final

They knew that if they could persuade the stadium authorities, the department of the environment, the fire department and the other powers that be, that it was practicable to race 500cc speedway machines on the glazed concrete surface of Wembley Arena, they were on a likely winner.

The Smallest Track In The World was marked out on the same surface where big fights, tennis tournaments, basketball, pop concerts and show jumping had taken place – measuring 118 yards. But before the go-ahead was given for the first Lada Indoor International, stringent tests had to be carried out.

Ian Thomas, co-promoter of the three indoor meetings that have taken place at Wembley Arena, explains: 'First of all we had to satisfy the Wembley authorities and the Speedway Control Board that indoor speedway was not some madcap idea. Did we have to lay a shale track? What about the noise, the fumes, the fire risk? Would the spectators be safe?

'Originally, we did toy with the idea of having a loose dirt surface but we decided against it for two reasons. One, the time factor. Wembley Arena is in great demand for all kinds of events and, though we made our plans well in advance, the date we were offered meant that we could not gain access to the arena until the actual day of the event. So there was no time to lay a dirt surface and try it out. Two, we decided the essence and appeal of indoor speedway was partly the fact that the spectators could sit in relative comfort under no threat from the weather and without being showered with shale.

'It was necessary to stage a practical demonstration to satisfy the authorities that it was possible to control a 500cc machine

This time the indoor action comes from Holland with Tommy Knudsen, John Louis and Steve Bastable providing the thrills. Could there be an indoor world championship in the near future? *Right* Jan Andersson . . . on the glazed concrete of Wembley Arena

on a miniature track. Decibel readings had to be taken to see whether the spectators would be deafened by the noise of the bikes. And, as a result, special silencers had to be fitted.

'Wembley Arena is fitted with fume extractors so that, in principle, solved one problem. Oil-catching trays, fitted to the bikes, were the solution to another. We couldn't afford to have oil patches on a slippery concrete surface. That would have been suicidal.

'But you can only go so far with tests. And, having been given the go-ahead, we set about publicising British speedway's first ever indoor speedway meeting, not knowing whether it would work or not.

'We booked some of the top riders in the world for a twenty-heat international individual event – and the tickets sold like hot cakes!

'I must say, at this point, that it was essential to have a major sponsor to make the event a practical proposition. The cost of staging a speedway event at Wembley Arena is colossal and when Ivan, Barry and myself, launched the first indoor show, we had no real idea of the public response.

'So Lada Cars took a massive gamble, just as we did. They were bold enough and adventurous enough to see the possibilities.'

Sunday 2 December 1979 was the big day and I well remember walking into the vast Wembley Arena during the morning practice session. I could not believe my eyes. As quickly as a rider came to the starting line and dropped the clutch, he ploughed into the boards. By midday, riders and machines were bruised and battered. No wonder, the track looked about the size of a postage stamp!

I had been employed as PRO for the event and it had not been difficult to sell. There is always a certain curiosity value with something new and the line-up was impressive . . . newly crowned world champion Ivan Mauger, runner-up Zenon Plech and that explosive little American star Kelly Moran plus a formidable list of international stars.

We had dreamed up a few gimmicks, too. All the officials, promoters, referee, announcer, etc, would wear full evening dress – just to prove that Indoor Speedway was clean enough for your Sunday best!

Now, an hour or two before the first race, panic gripped the promoters. The Wembley car park was filling up with cars and coaches, all the 7500 seats had been sold, yet inside the arena we had yet to risk four riders in one race. And when we did, no one stayed on long enough to finish it!

You couldn't blame the riders. One or two had a modicum of experience on indoor circuits around the world but the rest were venturing into the unknown.

Anyway, the doors opened, the band started to play and the first Lada Indoor International, pioneering indoor speedway in Britain, took to the track. What followed was a marvellous, crazy, laugh-a-minute, action-packed afternoon's entertainment which you either loved or hated.

In no way was it conventional speedway. Riders spun and slid into the straw bales and often, the ones who were lucky enough to stay aboard their bikes, found themselves heading in the wrong direction. There were spills galore and laughs aplenty. Nobody walked out!

And after twenty unbelievable heats, the old master Ivan Mauger emerged the victor with 13 points. No, it wasn't 'fixed'! Ivan may have had the occasional stroke of luck but he was smart enough to stay on his bike throughout his five rides and to keep picking up points. So the brilliant New Zealander added yet another prize to his vast collection.

The Wembley show divided the public. Some claimed the whole meeting was a farce, others went away delighted to have been entertained by something totally different. Both factions had valid arguments.

The *Daily* and *Sunday Mirror* sponsored a much more ambitious venture at the National Exhibition Centre in Birmingham soon after the Wembley event. Some of the racing was excellent but a complex formula and a meeting spread over three days, confused and irritated many of the spectators. Even so, it was a bold gamble and it enabled Sweden's Jan Andersson to make his first impact on the indoor scene.

Andersson won the individual event and the match-race competition. And he was at Wembley the following winter to score a 12-points maximum for the Rest of the World in a spectacular team event against Great Britain.

The normally placid Swede was angry about suggestions that he stole an unfair advantage in the second Lada Indoor International. It was widely reported that he had used a spray-on lacquer to enable his tyres to grip the glazed concrete surface. Andersson refuted the suggestion.

Either way, his superb solo performance could not save the Rest of the World from going down to a 40–38 last-heat defeat!

By now the promoters had realized the importance of making their Wembley winter show just that, a show. It wasn't enough to rely on the track action to entertain the family audience. And with Christmas being the festive season, who better to lead the grand parade than old Santa Claus himself?

The second Lada Indoor International was also highlighted by an interval demonstration of roller dancing, featuring England international Malcolm Simmons. When 'Simmo' swapped his bike and leathers for a natty shirt and a pair of roller skates the crowd got ready for a good laugh. But their chuckles turned to roars of appreciation as Simmo showed just how well he had mastered the technique of roller dancing.

Indoor speedway provides more than racing. It's a 'fun' afternoon and in 1981 Bruce Penhall joins in the Wembley Disco

So Wembley's winter indoor show had become established and the third Lada Indoor International took place on 29 November 1981 with another team event, Bruce Penhall's World Select against Peter Collins' Lions, as the centre-piece.

Somehow, this third show didn't quite ring the bell. Maybe the riders had become too adept at mastering the tiny polished track, maybe the teams were ill-matched because the Lions were not as strong as they might have been.

For the record, Bruce Penhall's Select won the team event 45–32 with Andersson unbeaten. And the Swede went on to win the King of the Concrete match-race title.

Andersson had come back to Wembley in the wake of a convincing win in an indoor meeting at Rotterdam. No wonder he was advocating that a World Indoor Championship might not be a bad idea!

With indoor speedway growing in popularity in Holland and West Germany there is, undoubtedly, scope for further development. Scottish international Jim McMillan, another accomplished performer, suggests the setting up of a European Indoor League.

Ian Thomas, co-promoter of the Lada meetings, says: 'It's an idea. But after our last Wembley show we have to have a re-think. The most important thing about an indoor show is to entertain the people, to give them variety, a nice mix of racing and off-beat attractions.

'The racing was not so exciting in 1981 at Wembley but the riders had learned how to cope with the problems of an indoor circuit. If we get too close to conventional speedway the indoor racing may lose some of its appeal.

'But indoor speedway is now established in Europe and there is no limit to the possibilities.'

King of the concrete
by Jan Andersson

The Swedish star who rides for Reading Racers in the British League, has become the established master of the art of indoor speedway . . . the Lada King of the Concrete. The only man to win the Swedish outdoor championship three times, he writes about his twin talents in this exclusive article.

Indoor speedway suits me more than conventional racing. I think, perhaps, I am not aggressive enough to be a world champion outdoors so I hope they will have an indoor world championship one day.

I like indoor racing because it is nice and clean. Some of the riders treat it as a joke but that is only because they cannot handle it. More and more are beginning to take it seriously.

The best indoor track I have seen is in Holland, in Rotterdam. It is wider than Wembley Arena where the Lada Indoor International is held, so there is more room for passing. But one of the races at Wembley in 1981, with Bruce Penhall and Steve Bastable, was very exciting and showed that it can be done.

I was very angry at Wembley in 1980. A lot of rubbish was talked about me after I scored a maximum there for the Rest of the World against Great Britain. I was supposed to have sprayed hair lacquer on my rear tyre to give me extra grip. In fact, all I did was to use a very fine oil spray on my *front* tyre. On indoor surfaces you get too much wheel grip at the back but very little at the front.

I was not the only rider to try this oil spray at the practice that year and I did not use it during the meeting because the referee decided not to allow it. So it was stupid to suggest that I had an unfair advantage or that the spray helped me to make the starts.

I think I can explain why I have been successful on the indoor circuits. I know how to prepare my engines for a very slick surface and how to take the wheel spin away. When I am at home in Sweden in the winter, I practise on a frozen lake near Gothenburg. I started doing that before the Mirror Group Newspapers indoor meeting at the National Exhibition Centre in Birmingham early in 1980. And I won both events – the *Daily Mirror* International Championship and the *Sunday Mirror* Match Race Championship.

On the ice, I mark out a small track and keep practising starts. You are probably wondering why I do not try ice speedway but it doesn't attract me at all.

The Birmingham track was bigger than Wembley and very fast. The surface was latex rubber whereas Wembley and Rotterdam are concrete.

How you set up your bike is very important. If you use high tyre pressure it makes the wheel spin. I have probably the lowest tyre pressure of any of the riders at

Wembley. I have also a crouching style because the bike is very difficult to handle on such a short track and you have to concentrate hard and be very steady. But I don't want to give all my secrets away . . . .

Some riders don't take indoor racing as seriously as I do. I spend a long time setting up my bikes. Before the 1981 Lada Indoor International I was up until 1 a.m. preparing my bike. As I said earlier, I was very angry about what had been written before the meeting and I was determined to prove I was good without any advantages. I was very happy when I scored maximum points again in the team match and won the King of the Concrete Match Race final. I think I proved my point.

I am twenty-seven years old and I have been riding speedway since 1974. I bought my first speedway bike in April of that year and won the Swedish Junior Championship four months later! Nothing I have done since has given me greater satisfaction. I didn't know much about speedway and I couldn't believe it when I won.

Before I had a go at speedway I raced 125 cc Yamahas on the road. I began to ride speedway for Kaparna of Gothenburg and came to England in 1975 on a tour of National League tracks. The next season I joined Swindon Robins in the British League and had three years with them before moving to Reading in 1979. That was the year I won the Swedish Championship for the first time and I have won it three years in a row, which is a record.

I am still with Kaparna but I have a house in England now and love it here.

I enjoy riding in the British League and usually have my best spell in the first three months of the season. I feel hungrier for success after a good rest in the winter.

I don't want to be the world champion desperately like some other riders. It is a very hard thing to do and perhaps I don't put enough work in. Every year I find it harder to work on my bikes. I do not have any mechanics because I have never wanted to let anybody else do my engines.

Maybe I don't work so hard because I know I can do quite well without that extra effort.

I thought I had quite a good chance of winning the world final in Gothenburg in 1980 because it was on my home track. If they had kept the track with plenty of dirt as it is normally, I might have won. I could not believe it when they changed it. I had set all my engines up for the usual track, but it was very hard and slick. I am sure the Swedish authorities did not think at all about trying to prepare the track for me, even though I was the only Swedish rider in the final and we have not had a champion since Anders Michanek, in 1974.

I did well in Gothenburg apart from one ride, in heat 5 when I drew gate three, which was very poor for everybody. I finished last behind Michael Lee, Bruce Penhall and Billy Sanders, but dropped only one more point all night. So I was fourth overall with 11 points.

I did not expect to do well at Wembley in 1981. I was having a down period and, although a lot of people helped me that night, nothing worked.

I keep very busy riding in the Swedish and British Leagues. It would be good to see Sweden come back as a force in international speedway but it will take at least another five years. We have some good young riders coming up, and the crowds are starting to improve. We will have to see. Meanwhile I am planning to work a bit harder and perhaps 1982 will be my best season in British League. I hope so.

Mauger anniversary!

It is twenty-five years since Ivan Mauger made his first appearance in British speedway. He was young, ambitious and penniless. Now, a quarter of a century on, he can look back with pride on a career that has brought him every conceivable honour in the sport and a record six world individual championships, **nine** *if you count his successes in the World Long-track event.* **Richard Bott** *pays this tribute to the ageless New Zealander.*

Well, it's supposed to be *my* tribute but I can't think of a better opening line than one Ivan came out with as we looked back over his career at the end of last season. He told me: 'In twenty-five years I've never done anything that's been expected of me . . . apart from win things!'

Great champions are rarely humble when it comes to the nitty gritty. Their strength is that they believe they are the best. They don't need someone to pat them on the back and say 'Good luck'. You can pat them on the back when they've won!

And great champions go on winning. I was thumbing through the pages of Ivan's autobiography *Triple Crown Plus*, published by Pelham Books in 1971. Naturally, it carried chapter and verse on his first world title triumph, at the Ullevi Stadium, Gothenburg, in 1968. What I liked, particularly, was the start of the next chapter. It read: 'Having won the world title once, what was there left? The answer, simply . . . another world final!'

You only have to look at any current record book to see just what this remarkable New Zealander meant. He went on winning . . . and winning . . . and winning.

And not just winning races, either. Winning battles. Over the years, Ivan has never been afraid to speak his mind, to say to hell with convention and protocol. Introduced to the crowd before one British League Riders' Championship meeting at Belle Vue, several years ago, he took the microphone and complained bitterly to the crowd about the seating arrangements for the riders' wives!

When he smashed his ankle in nine places in last year's World Long-track Championship final in Radgona, Yugoslavia, he had the ideal opportunity to hang up his leathers. Nobody would have blamed him. Just short of his forty-second birthday, his cupboards and cabinets stuffed with every kind of trophy under the sun, he was ripe for retirement. Or so it seemed.

Above **Flashback to 1969 . . . Ivan Mauger's second world title and he is pictured with the famous winged wheel that has become his personal property**
Below **Flashback to 1970 . . . Ivan the incredible triumphs again, this time in Poland, becoming the first three-time winner**

But within a few weeks he was hobbling around on crutches, paying twice-daily trips to the physiotherapist and talking about the 1982 World Championship. Not just talking but preparing to ride in it.

'I'll retire when I'm good and ready,' he snapped. 'Not when anyone else says I should. If I had retired when everybody thought I should have done, in the mid-seventies, I'd have only four world titles. Now I've got six – and I'd like seven!'

The world crown was always the jewel on his horizon from the minute he arrived in England to a fanfare of trumpets, in 1957. Born in Christchurch, New Zealand, the city that produced two other great champions, Ronnie Moore and Barry Briggs, Ivan was given the big build-up when he joined Wimbledon as a seventeen-year-old.

Mind you, he had done his own drum-beating back in New Zealand, announcing that he was about to sail for England and take British speedway by storm. He had seen his idol, Ronnie Moore, come home with all the trappings of success and believed the same riches were waiting for him in England. They were . . . but not for a few years.

Married at sixteen and with his first child on the way, Ivan breezed into London with his wife Raye, ready for the start of the 1957 season. But he soon found out that there are no short cuts to the top.

The novelty of seeing his name in the headlines soon wore off when Wimbledon couldn't find a place for him in their line-up and he was happy to earn £7 a week as a groundsman to supplement anything he made from a few second-half rides. The 'new Ronnie Moore' found himself turning out for Rye House in the Southern Area League!

The Maugers lived in a tiny flat in Wimbledon and Ivan rode an old bike that he used to paint silver before every meeting, so it would look a bit better than it was! Now he has a priceless gold-plated bike which he shows off at exhibitions all around the world.

So there was no story-book start for the precocious kid from Christchurch, just a salutary lesson in the hard facts of life. His daughter Julie was born and during the winter of 1957–58, Ivan had to take a job as a milkman to keep the wolf from the door.

In 1958, Ivan was loaned out to Eastbourne and at last began to look the part. But he was becoming disillusioned with English speedway and headed home to New Zealand at the end of the season. We didn't see him again until 1963!

Ivan turned his attention to Australia for a few years and by now had added Kym and Debbie to his family. He began to blossom as a rider while he was based in Adelaide and it fired his ambition again. He wondered if he could go back to England and succeed at the second attempt. But somebody would have to pay his and his family's fare.

Somebody did. Newcastle Diamonds promoter Mike Parker sent Ivan a telegram in reply to the rider's request to return to England. And he came up with the money. So the Mauger family set sail for Southampton early in 1963.

'I was beginning my career all over again,' said Ivan. 'I had been a star-struck youngster in 1957. Now I was more than a little apprehensive about whether I would be good enough.'

Based in Manchester, an area he has come to love, Ivan soon established himself at Newcastle and carried off the Provincial

What's on Ivan's mind . . . another world title?

League Riders' championship at Belle Vue in his first season back in this country. At last he began to believe in those boyhood dreams . . . and the world championship! Gradually, the thought of that glittering prize became an obsession.

Not even a broken ankle could keep Ivan out of the qualifying rounds in 1965 but it was the following season when he made his mark, winning the European championship at Wembley and finishing a very creditable fourth in his first world final, in Sweden. But even that left a sour taste in Ivan's mouth. He was unable to ride in the world final practice because of a Newcastle commitment and that led to bitter arguments with Mike Parker, the promoter who had brought him back to Britain. It was the beginning of a feud which was to lead to his departure from Newcastle.

But Mauger was still a Newcastle rider in 1967, when a heavy spill at Wembley – Sweden's Bernie Persson crashed into him – wrecked his hopes when he was sure he was set for victory. This time he had to settle for third place. But he was getting closer!

From the dawning of New Year's Day, 1968, Ivan Mauger's singleminded ambition was to become world champion. He was angry that the title had been snatched from his grasp the previous year. He was at loggerheads with Mike Parker. He was in no mood to settle for second best.

Having switched allegiance from the British built JAP engine to the Czechoslovakian Jawa, Ivan was in spellbinding form, winning the British and British-Nordic finals. But he was after the star prize and, in Gothenburg, he lifted it. A month before his twenty-ninth birthday he was world champion. It had been a long wait but he was about to make up for those unfulfilled years.

Having signed a contract to ride for the Jawa factory, Ivan now had the quality equipment and the world title to kick open a few doors. One of them was Newcastle's and off he went to join Belle Vue Aces. If Newcastle had tried to keep him he would have quit the sport!

Happily ensconced at Belle Vue, virtually on his doorstep, Ivan went from strength to strength. World champion again at Wembley in 1969 . . . and for a third time in Wroclaw in 1970. He became the first rider in history to win the title three years in succession. One of his rewards? That magnificent gold-plated bike.

'To be honest,' says Ivan, 'I can't understand why nobody won it three times in a row years before I did. It was virtually the British Riders' championship when it was held at Wembley during the forties and fifties.

'Wroclaw 1970, my third title, will always be special to me. Not just because it was the third time but because of the level of competition, and the venue. Eight or nine Eastern Europeans were good enough to win that day.

'Add myself, Ole Olsen, Anders Michanek and Barry Briggs and you get an idea of the competition. England's Trevor Hedge was, probably, the only rider in the final who wasn't fancied at all – yet he helped me to win it!

'The Poles had a reserve called Edmund Migos, who was as good as the riders they had in the final. He came in and won two races . . . by a mile! He was due out again in my last race because "Hedgey" had crashed and was badly shaken up.

'I was off gate three and Migos would have been inside me, next to Antoni Woryna, one of the other Poles. So I talked Hedgey into riding, even though he was in so much pain he couldn't fasten his helmet.

'I told him "I don't want Migos in this race. Just make the start and then fall off or stop." So he lined up and I made the best start I've ever made in my life. I was under so much pressure with a third consecutive title resting on that one race.'

Even three in a row wasn't enough for Ivan and he has gone on acquiring world titles, international and domestic awards ever since. At the last count he had accumulated thirty FIM gold medals and certificates and something in the region of 3000 trophies, medals and souvenirs.

World title No. 4 came at Wembley in 1972, No. 5 at Gothenburg in 1977 and No. 6 – smashing Ove Fundin's record – at Katowice in 1979. Whether there are any more on the horizon remains to be seen.

Certainly there should have been more. He goofed in Katowice in 1973 when Poland's Jerzy Szczakiel defeated him in a run-off for the title. For once the ice-cool Kiwi made his move too soon and fell on the pits turn. That is the only occasion I can ever remember him blaming himself for a defeat.

In the last few years he has suffered from back trouble and a blood disorder, the latter by far the more serious problem. As Ivan says: 'If you walk around with your arm in plaster or hobble about on crutches, people sympathize because they can see that something is wrong. But with a blood disorder, or back trouble, there is no visible evidence of discomfort and nobody sympathizes.

'Gordon Kennett is a classic case. He was blamed for loss of form and lack of effort and then they found he was diabetic. No wonder he was always feeling jaded.'

Ivan apologizes for falling short of his own high standards in the last couple of years and insists it is not down to old age.

'While the blood disorder was affecting me, I could hardly raise the enthusiasm to ride. I was filling myself up with pills and, several times, I had to visit my local hospital to take a blood test before I set off to ride in a meeting!

'My only value to Hull in the last two years was whatever points I managed to score. Previously, I had helped to get the best out of the other riders by making sure they had the right gear ratio and generally advising them. While I was ill I had neither the strength nor the enthusiasm for that. Sometimes I felt so lethargic after a meeting that it was an effort to get dressed.

'I am getting older and I accept that whereas I used to be able to win meetings using 80 per cent of my ability, I now have to use 100 per cent. But I believe I am good enough to win more world championships, particularly the long-track, provided I am in good health.

'I get ribbed in the dressing room by the young guys who call me "grandad" and that sort of thing. But I've got a stock answer. I tell them, "If you are very careful and take care of yourself and are extremely lucky, you might just get to be as old as me. Millions of people never live to see 40!" It's amazing how people seem to think there is a stigma about growing old. I reckon it's a privilege.'

The amazing New Zealander regards 1972 as his 'golden year'. He won three world finals, individual, team (as Great Britain's skipper) and long-track. And he was also involved in a run-off for the pairs championship. 'Yes, I nearly did the grand slam on my own that year!' he quips.

'That was my best year because I had a broken scaphoid – but it only hurt when I was riding!'

Mauger's career has not only been a story of personal achievement but of inspiration and leadership with club and country.

When Great Britain did not have the quality of rider to challenge for the world team title, Mauger and his fellow New Zealander Barry Briggs led them to it. More recently, in 1979, it gave him immense satisfaction, after being discarded by England, to inspire New Zealand to win the team title on their own.

At club level he has moulded every one of his teams into a potent force . . . Newcastle, Belle Vue, Exeter and Hull.

As an ambassador for the sport he has broken down barriers, rid speedway of its grease-and-grime image, introduced showmanship and style without losing any of his professionalism and, it has to be said, made himself thoroughly unpopular in certain quarters by being prepared to kick the sport's establishment in the teeth.

He argues, with a good deal of justification, that he only gets publicity when he is controversial.

But his record is incomparable. He may not be the greatest rider of all time but no one can match his haul of trophies or his durability. Others won the world championship at a younger age, others were and are more spectacular, others went on riding until they were fifty. Maybe Ivan will, though I very much doubt it.

What is beyond all reasonable doubt, is that in twenty-five years he has become the best-known, highest-paid, most consistently successful, most talked about, filmed and photographed individual in the sport.

And, one way or another, I wager he'll be making headlines for the next twenty-five years, too!

World championship check-out

Individual competition

1936 (Wembley)	1 Lionel Van Praag (Australia)	26 pts*
	2 Eric Langton (England)	26 pts
	3 'Bluey' Wilkinson (Australia)	25 pts
1937 (Wembley)	1 Jack Milne (USA)	28 pts
	2 Wilbur Lamoreaux (USA)	25 pts
	3 Cordy Milne (USA)	23 pts
1938 (Wembley)	1 'Bluey' Wilkinson (Australia)	22 pts
	2 Jack Milne (USA)	21 pts
	3 Wilbur Lamoreaux (USA)	20 pts
1939–1948	No final held	
1949 (Wembley)	1 Tommy Price (England)	15 pts
	2 Jack Parker (England)	14 pts
	3 Louis Lawson (England)	13 pts
1950 (Wembley)	1 Freddie Williams (Wales)	14 pts
	2 Wally Green (England)	13 pts
	3 Graham Warren (Australia)	12 pts
1951 (Wembley)	1 Jack Young (Australia)	12 pts*
	2 Split Waterman (England)	12 pts
	3 Jack Biggs (Australia)	12 pts
1952 (Wembley)	1 Jack Young (Australia)	14 pts
	2 Freddie Williams (Wales)	13 pts
	3 Bob Oakley (England)	12 pts
1953 (Wembley)	1 Freddie Williams (Wales)	14 pts
	2 Split Waterman (England)	13 pts
	3 Geoff Mardon (New Zealand)	12 pts*
1954 (Wembley)	1 Ronnie Moore (New Zealand)	15 pts
	2 Brian Crutcher (England)	13 pts*
	3 Olle Nygren (Sweden)	13 pts
1955 (Wembley)	1 Peter Craven (England)	13 pts
	2 Ronnie Moore (New Zealand)	12 pts*
	3 Barry Briggs (New Zealand)	12 pts
1956 (Wembley)	1 Ove Fundin (Sweden)	13 pts
	2 Ronnie Moore (New Zealand)	12 pts
	3 Arthur Forrest (England)	11 pts
1957 (Wembley)	1 Barry Briggs (New Zealand)	14 pts*
	2 Ove Fundin (Sweden)	14 pts
	3 Peter Craven (England)	11 pts*
1958 (Wembley)	1 Barry Briggs (New Zealand)	15 pts
	2 Ove Fundin (Sweden)	13 pts
	3 Aub Lawson (Australia)	11 pts*
1959 (Wembley)	1 Ronnie Moore (New Zealand)	15 pts
	2 Ove Fundin (Sweden)	13 pts
	3 Barry Briggs (New Zealand)	11 pts*
1960 (Wembley)	1 Ove Fundin (Sweden)	14 pts*
	2 Ronnie Moore (New Zealand)	14 pts
	3 Peter Craven (England)	14 pts
1961 (Malmo)	1 Ove Fundin (Sweden)	14 pts
	2 Bjorn Knutsson (Sweden)	12 pts*
	3 Gote Nordin (Sweden)	12 pts
1962 (Wembley)	1 Peter Craven (England)	14 pts
	2 Barry Briggs (New Zealand)	13 pts
	3 Ove Fundin (Sweden)	10 pts*
1963 (Wembley)	1 Ove Fundin (Sweden)	14 pts
	2 Bjorn Knutsson (Sweden)	13 pts
	3 Barry Briggs (New Zealand)	12 pts
1964 (Gothenburg)	1 Barry Briggs (New Zealand)	15 pts
	2 Igor Plechanov (USSR)	13 pts*
	3 Ove Fundin (Sweden)	13 pts
1965 (Wembley)	1 Bjorn Knutsson (Sweden)	14 pts
	2 Igor Plechanov (USSR)	13 pts*
	3 Ove Fundin (Sweden)	13 pts
1966 (Gothenburg)	1 Barry Briggs (New Zealand)	15 pts
	2 Sverre Harrfeldt (Norway)	14 pts
	3 Antoni Woryna (Poland)	13 pts
1967 (Wembley)	1 Ove Fundin (Sweden)	14 pts*
	2 Bengt Jansson (Sweden)	14 pts
	3 Ivan Mauger (New Zealand)	13 pts
1968 (Gothenburg)	1 Ivan Mauger (New Zealand)	15 pts
	2 Barry Briggs (New Zealand)	12 pts
	3 Edward Jancarz (Poland)	11 pts*

The kind of action to get the fans roaring. Dave Jessup storms out in front of Ian Cartwright, John Louis and Scott Autrey in the Overseas final at White City

1969 (Wembley)	1 Ivan Mauger (New Zealand)	14 pts	1975 (Wembley)	1 Ole Olsen (Denmark)	15 pts
	2 Barry Briggs (New Zealand)	11 pts*		2 Anders Michanek (Sweden)	13 pts
	3 Soren Sjosten (Sweden)	11 pts		3 John Louis (England)	12 pts*
1970 (Wroclaw)	1 Ivan Mauger (New Zealand)	15 pts	1976 (Katowice)	1 Peter Collins (England)	14 pts
	2 Pawel Waloszek (Poland)	14 pts		2 Malcolm Simmons (England)	13 pts
	3 Antoni Woryna (Poland)	13 pts		3 Phil Crump (Australia)	12 pts
1971 (Gothen-burg)	1 Ole Olsen (Denmark)	15 pts	1977 (Gothen-burg)	1 Ivan Mauger (New Zealand)	14 pts
	2 Ivan Mauger (New Zealand)	12 pts*		2 Peter Collins (England)	13 pts
	3 Bengt Jansson (Sweden)	12 pts		3 Ole Olsen (Denmark)	12 pts*
1972 (Wembley)	1 Ivan Mauger (New Zealand)	13 pts*	1978 (Wembley)	1 Ole Olsen (Denmark)	13 pts
	2 Bernt Persson (Sweden)	13 pts		2 Gordon Kennett (England)	12 pts
	3 Ole Olsen (Denmark)	12 pts		3 Scott Autrey (USA)	11 pts
1973 (Katowice)	1 Jerzy Szczakiel (Poland)	13 pts*	1979 (Katowice)	1 Ivan Mauger (New Zealand)	14 pts
	2 Ivan Mauger (New Zealand)	13 pts		2 Zenon Plech (Poland)	13 pts
	3 Zenon Plech (Poland)	12 pts		3 Michael Lee (England)	11 pts*
1974 (Gothen-burg)	1 Anders Michanek (Sweden)	15 pts	1980 (Gothen-burg)	1 Michael Lee (England	14 pts
	2 Ivan Mauger (New Zealand)	11 pts		2 Dave Jessup (England)	12 pts*
	3 Soren Sjosten (Sweden)	11 pts		3 Billy Sanders (Australia)	12 pts

1981 Wembley

BRUCE PENHALL (USA)	3	3	3	3	2	14 pts
Ole Olsen (Denmark)	2	2	3	2	3	12 *
Tommy Knudsen (Denmark)	3	2	2	2	3	12
Kenny Carter (England)	3	2	3	ef	3	11
Erik Gundersen (Denmark)	2	3	0	3	3	11
Jan Andersson (Sweden)	1	2	1	3	2	9
Egon Muller (West Germany)	1	1	3	2	2	9
Dave Jessup (England)	3	3	ef	ef	1	7
Hans Nielsen (Denmark)	2	0	0	2	2	6
Michael Lee (England)	0	3	2	0	F	5
Chris Morton (England)	2	1	1	1	0	5
Edward Jancarz (Poland)	1	1	1	1	1	5
Larry Ross (New Zealand)	0	ex	1	3	0	4
Zenon Plech (Poland)	F	0	2	1	0	3
Ales Dryml (Czechoslovakia)	0	0	2	0	1	3
Jiri Stancl (Czechoslovakia)	1	1	0	0	1	3
Henryk Olszak (Poland – reserve)	one ride, no points					

(* after a run-off)

Team Competition

1960: Gothenburg, Sweden
SWEDEN 44 (O. Fundin 12, O. Nygren 12,
R. Sormander 11, B. Knutsson 9)
England 30 (P. Craven 8, K. McKinlay 8, R. How 7,
G. White 6, N. Boocock 1)
Czechoslovakia 15 (A. Kasper 5, L. Tomicek 4,
F. Richetr 3, J. Mahac 3)
Poland 7 (K. Pociejkowicz 3, M. Kaiser 2, M. Polukard
2, J. Malinowski 0)

1961: Wroclaw, Poland
POLAND 32 (M. Kaiser 10, H. Zyto 7, F. Kapala 6,
M. Polukard 5, S. Tkocz 4)
Sweden 31 (O. Fundin 11, R. Sormander 10,
B. Knutsson 7, P. T. Svensson 3)
England 21 (P. Craven 8, Andrews 6, K. McKinlay 4,
R. How 3)
Czechoslovakia 12 (L. Tomicek 7, A. Kasper 4,
B. Bartonek 1, M. Svoboda 0)

1962: Slany, Czechoslovakia
SWEDEN 36 (B. Knutsson 10, S. Sjosten 10, O. Fundin
9, G. Nordin 4, R. Sormander 3)
Gt. Britain 24 (R. Moore 10, B. Briggs 8, P. Craven 6,
R. Hoɪ 0, C. Maidment 0)
Poland 20 (M. Kaiser 9, F. Kapala 5, J. Maj 4,
P. Waloszek 2, M. Polukard 0)
Czechoslovakia 16 (L. Tomicek 7, B. Slany 4, J. Volf 3,
J. Prusa 2)

1963: Vienna, Austria
SWEDEN 37 (B. Knutsson 11, P.O. Soederman 10,
O. Fundin 7, G. Nordin 6, R. Sormander 3)
Czechoslovakia 27 (A. Kasper 10, S. Kubicek 7,
L. Tomicek 5, M. Smid 5)
Gt. Britain 25 (B. Briggs 12, P. Craven 8, D. Fisher 4,
R. Moore 1)
Poland 7 (H. Zyto 4, M. Kaiser 1, S. Tcokz 1, J. Maj 1,
A. Pogorzelski 0)

1964: Abensberg, Germany
SWEDEN 34 (B. Knutsson 11, G. Nordin 10,
R. Sormander 7, O. Fundin 6)
U.S.S.R. 25 (I. Plechanov 8, G. Kurilenko 8,
Y. Chekranov 6, B. Samorodov 3)
Gt. Britain 21 (B. Briggs 9, K. McKinlay 7, N. Boocock
3, R. How 2, B. Brett 0)
Poland 16 (A. Wyglenda 8, Z. Podlecki 3,
A. Pogorzelski 3, M. Rose 2, M. Kaiser 0)

1965: Kempten, W. Germany
POLAND 38 (A. Pogorzelski 11, A. Wyglenda 11,
A. Woryna 9, Z. Podlecki 7)
Sweden 33 (B. Knutsson 11, O. Fundin 8, B. Jansson 8,
G. Nordin 6)
Gt. Britain 18 (K. McKinlay 7, N. Boocock 6, J. Gooch
3, B. Briggs 1, C. Monk 1)
U.S.S.R. 7 (Y. Chekranov 2, G. Kurilenko 2,
V. Sokolov 2, I. Plechanov 1, V. Trofimov 0)

1966: Wroclaw, Poland
POLAND 40 (A. Wyglenda 11, A. Woryna 11, M. Rose
10, A. Pogorzelski 8)
U.S.S.R. 26 (B. Samorodov 10, V. Trofimov 6,
I. Plechanov 6, F. Szajnuvov 4)
Sweden 22 (B. Knutsson 11, L. Enecrona 4, G. Nordin
3, O. Fundin 2, L. Larsson 2)
Gt. Britain 8 (N. Boocock 4, I. Mauger 3, B. Briggs 1,
C. Pratt 0, T. Betts 0)

1967: Malmo, Sweden
SWEDEN 32 (G. Nordin 11, B. Jansson 9, O. Fundin 6,
T. Harrysson 6)
Poland 26 (A. Woryna 10, A. Wyglenda 9,
J. Trzeszowski 4, Z. Podlecki 3, A. Pogorzelski 0)
Gt. Britain 19 (B. Briggs 8, E. Boocock 5, Ray Wilson 4,
I. Mauger 2, C. Pratt 0)
U.S.S.R. 19 (I. Plechanov 9, V. Trofimov 4,
B. Samorodov 3, G. Kadirov 2, F. Szajnuvov 1)

1968: Wembley, England
GT. BRITAIN 40 (I. Mauger 12, N. Boocock 10,
M. Ashby 8, B. Briggs 7, N. Hunter 3)
Sweden 30 (O. Fundin 11, A. Michanek 7, B. Jansson 7,
O. Nygren 3, T. Harrysson 2)
Poland 19 (E. Migos 8, E. Jancarz 6, A. Wyglenda 2,
H. Gluklich 2, P. Waloszek 1)
Czechoslovakia 7 (A. Kasper 3, L. Tomicek 2, J. Volf 1,
J. Holub 1)

1969: Rybnik, Poland

POLAND 31 (E. Jancarz 11, A. Wyglenda 11, S. Tkocz 4, H. Gluklich 3, A. Pogorzelski 2)

Gt. Britain 27 (I. Mauger 9, B. Briggs 8, N. Boocock 5, M. Ashby 5)

U.S.S.R. 23 (V. Smirnov 9, G. Kurilenko 8, V. Klementiev 5, Y. Dubinin 1, V. Trofimov 0)

Sweden 12 (A. Michanek 7, S. Sjosten 2, O. Fundin 2, B. Jansson 1)

1970: Wembley, England

SWEDEN 42 (O. Fundin 11, B. Jansson 11, A. Michanek 10, S. Sjosten 10)

Gt. Britain 31 (B. Briggs 11, I. Mauger 9, E. Boocock 5, Ray Wilson 4, N. Boocock 2)

Poland 20 (J. Mucha 6, A. Woryna 5, E. Migos 4, H. Gluklich 3, P. Waloszek 2)

Czechoslovakia 3 (V. Verner 3, Z. Majstr 0, M. Verner 0, J. Stancl 0, J. Holub 0)

1971: Wroclaw, Poland

GT. BRITAIN 37 (Ray Wilson 12, I. Mauger 10, J. Airey 9, B. Briggs 6)

U.S.S.R. 22 (G. Chlinovski 8, V. Smirnov 7, Vlad Gordeev 4, A. Kuzmin 3)

Poland 19 (H. Gluklich 6, P. Waloszek 5, A. Woryna 4. E. Jancarz 4)

Sweden 18 (A. Michanek 9, S. Sjosten 3, B. Jansson 3, L. Enecrona 3, B. Persson 0)

1972: Olching, W. Germany

GT. BRITAIN 36 (I. Mauger 11, J. Louis 9, T. Betts 8, Ray Wilson 8)

U.S.S.R. 21 (A. Kuzmin 6, G. Chlinovski 5, V. Kalmikov 5, V. Trofimov 5)

Poland 21 (Z. Plech 7, H. Gluklich 6, P. Waloszek 5, O. Dombrowski 3, M. Cieslak 0)

Sweden 18 (C. Lofqvist 6, A. Michanek 4, T. Jansson 4, J. Simensen 3, G. Nordin 1)

1973: Wembley, England

GT. BRITAIN 37 (P. Collins 12, T. Betts 9, Ray Wilson 8, M. Simmons 8)

Sweden 31 (A. Michanek 11, B. Persson 9, B. Jansson 6, T. Jansson 5)

U.S.S.R. 20 (Vladimir Gordeev 7, V. Paznikov 5, G. Chlinovski 4, A. Pavlov 2, V. Trofimov 2)

Poland 8 (Z. Plech 5, E. Jancarz 2, P. Waloszek 1, J. Szczakiel 0)

1974: Katowice, Poland

ENGLAND 42 (P. Collins 12, J. Louis 12, D. Jessup 10, M. Simmons 8)

Sweden 31 (S. Sjosten 10, A. Michanek 9, T. Jansson 7, C. Lofqvist 5)

Poland 13 (J. Mucha 4, Z. Plech 4, A. Jurczynski 3, A. Tkocz 2, J. Szczakiel 0)

U.S.S.R. 10 (M. Krasnov 5, Vlad Gordeev 4, W. Kalmiskov 1, A. Kuzmin 0)

1975: Norden, W. Germany

ENGLAND 41 (P. Collins 12, M. Simmons 11, M. Ashby 10, J. Louis 8)

U.S.S.R. 29 (Val Gordeev 8, G. Chlinovski 8, V. Trofimov 8, Vlad Gordeev 5)

Sweden 17 (A. Michanek 8, T. Jansson 4, B. Persson 2, S. Sjosten 2, S. Karlsson 1)

Poland 9 (M. Cieslak 4, J. Rembas 2, M. Gluklich 2, E. Jancarz 1, Z. Plech 0)

1976: White City, England

AUSTRALIA 31 (P. Crump 11, B. Sanders 7, P. Herne 7, J. Boulger 6)

Poland 28 (E. Jancarz 9, M. Cieslak 7, Z. Plech 6, J. Rembas 5, B. Proch 1)

Sweden 26 (A. Michanek 11, B. Persson 8, L. A. Andersson 5, B. Jansson 1, C. Lofqvist 1)

U.S.S.R. 11 (Val Gordeev 5, G. Chlinovski 2, Vlad Gordeev 2, V. Paznikov 2, V. Trofimov 0)

1977: Wroclaw, Poland

ENGLAND 37 (P. Collins 10, D. Jessup 9, M. Lee 9, J. Davis 6, M. Simmons 3)

Poland 25 (E. Jancarz 10, B. Nowak 6, J. Rembas 6, M. Cieslak 2, R. Fabiszewski 1)

Czechoslovakia 23 (J. Stancl 8, A. Dryml 5, V. Verner 5, J. Verner 5)

Sweden 11 (A. Michanek 5, B. Persson 4, B. Jansson 2, T. Nilsson 0, S. Karlsson 0)

1978: Landshut, W. Germany

DENMARK 37 (H. Nielsen 11, O. Olsen 10, M. Lohmann 9, F. Thomsen 7)

England 27 (M. Simmons 8, P. Collins 6, M. Lee 5, D. Jessup 5, G. Kennett 3)

Poland 16 (E. Jancarz 6, M. Cieslak 5, J. Rembas 3, Z. Plech 1, A. Huszcza 1)

Czechoslovakia 16 (J. Stancl 7, J. Verner 5, V. Verner 2, A. Dryml 2)

1979: White City, England

NEW ZEALAND 35 (L. Ross 11, M. Shirra 10, I. Mauger 9, B. Cribb 5)

Denmark 31 (O. Olsen 12, H. Nielsen 9, M. Lohmann 6, F. Thomsen 4, B. Petersen 0)

Czechoslovakia 19 (J. Stancl 6, A. Dryml 5, Z. Kudrna 4, V. Verner 4)

Poland 11 (P. Pyszny 4, Z. Plech 4, R. Slabon 2, M. Cieslak 1, A. Tkocz 0)

1980: Wroclaw, Poland

ENGLAND 40 (C. Morton 11, M. Lee 11, P. Collins 10, D. Jessup 8, J. Davis, reserve, did not ride)

USA 29 (B. Penhall 12, S. Autrey 9, D. Sigalos 5, B. Schwartz 3, R. Preston, reserve, 0)

Poland 15 (Z. Plech 5, R. Jankowski 5, E. Jancarz 3, A. Huszcza 2, J. Rembas, reserve, 0)

Czechoslovakia 12 (J. Stancl 4, J. Verner 3, P. Ondrasik 3, A. Dryml 1, Z. Kudrna, reserve, 2)

1981: Olching, West Germany

1 DENMARK 36 (Hans Nielsen 11, Erik Gundersen 9, Tommy Knudsen 9, Ole Olsen 6, Finn Thomsen, reserve, 1)

2 ENGLAND 29 (Chris Morton 11, Kenny Carter 9, John Davis 5, Dave Jessup 3, Gordon Kennett, reserve, 1)

3 WEST GERMANY 28 (Egon Muller 10, Karl Maier 8, Georg Hack 5, Georg Gilgenreiner 5)

4 USSR 3 (Victor Kuznekov 2, Nikolai Kornev 1, Vladimir Gordeev 0, Mikhail Starostin 0, Alexi Maximov, reserve, 0)

Pairs championship

1968: Kempten, West Germany
SWEDEN (Ove Fundin 14, Torbjorn Harrysson 10) 24 pts, Great Britain (Geoff Mudge 12, Ray Wilson 9) 21, Norway (Odd Fossengen 11, Oyvind Berg 5) 16

1969: Stockholm, Sweden
NEW ZEALAND (Ivan Mauger 18, Bob Andrews 10) 28 pts, Sweden (Ove Fundin 14, Gote Nordin 13) 27, England (Nigel Boocock 11, Martin Ashby 10) 21

1970: Malmo, Sweden
NEW ZEALAND (Ronnie Moore 16, Ivan Mauger 12) 28 pts, Sweden (Ove Fundin 15, Bengt Jansson 10) 25, England (Eric Boocock 13, Nigel Boocock 6) 19

1971: Rybnik, Poland
POLAND (Jerzy Szczakiel 16, Andrzej Wyglenda 14) 30 pts, New Zealand (Barry Briggs 14, Ivan Mauger 11) 25, Sweden (Anders Michanek 13, Bernt Persson 9) 22

1972: Boras, Sweden
ENGLAND (Ray Wilson 15, Terry Betts 9) 24 pts,* New Zealand (Ivan Mauger 14, Ronnie Moore 10) 24, Sweden 'B' (Bernt Persson 13, Hasse Holmqvist 0) 22.
*Wilson beat Mauger in match race run-off for title

1973: Boras, Sweden
SWEDEN (Anders Michanek 15, Tommy Jansson 9) 24, Denmark (Ole Olsen 18, Kurt Bogh 3) 21, Poland (Zenon Plech 14, Zbignien Marcinkowski 7) 21

1974: Manchester, England
SWEDEN (Anders Michanek 14, Soren Sjosten 14) 28 pts, Australia (Phil Crump 14, John Boulger 9) 23, New Zealand (Ivan Mauger 17, Barry Briggs 4) 21

1975: Wroclaw, Poland
SWEDEN (Anders Michanek 17, Tommy Jansson 7) 24 pts, Poland (Edward Jancarz 15, Pawel Bruzda 8) 23, Denmark (Ole Olsen 18, Jan Henningsen 2) 20

1976: Eskilstuna, Sweden
ENGLAND (John Louis 17, Malcolm Simmons 10) 27 pts, Denmark (Ole Olsen 16, Finn Thomsen 8) 24, Sweden (Bengt Jansson 11, Bernt Persson 11) 22

1977: Manchester, England
ENGLAND (Peter Collins 15, Malcolm Simmons 13) 28 pts, Sweden (Anders Michanek 16, Bernt Persson 2) 18, West Germany (Egon Muller 11, Hans Wassermann 7) 18

1978: Katowice, Poland
ENGLAND (Malcolm Simmons 15, Gordon Kennett 9) 24 pts*, New Zealand (Ivan Mauger 12, Larry Ross 12) 24, Denmark (Ole Olsen 16, Finn Thomsen 5) 21.
*Simmons beat Mauger in match race run-off for title

1979: Vojens, Denmark
DENMARK (Ole Olsen 15, Hans Nielsen 10) 25 pts, England (Michael Lee 15, Malcolm Simmons 9) 24, Poland (Edward Jancarz 14, Zenon Plech 6) 20

1980: Krsko, Yugoslavia
ENGLAND 29 (Dave Jessup 16, Peter Collins 13), Poland 22 (Edward Jancarz 16, Zenon Plech 6), Denmark 21 (Ole Olsen 13, Hans Nielsen 8)

1981: Katowice, Poland

1 USA 23 (Bruce Penhall 14, Bobby Schwartz 9)

2 NEW ZEALAND 22 (Ivan Mauger 12, Larry Ross 10)

3 POLAND 21 (Zenon Plech 15, Edward Jancarz 6)

4 CZECHOSLOVAKIA 18 (Ales Dryml 12, Jan Verner 6)

5 ENGLAND 17 (Chris Morton 10, Dave Jessup 7)

6 DENMARK 17 (Ole Olsen 10, Hans Nielsen 7)

7 WEST GERMANY 3 (Egon Muller 2, Georg Gilgenreiner 1)